Legalised Robbery

How Insolvency Practitioners Stole Britain's Future

By Patrick Donnelly

This book is dedicated to all the resilient and brave souls who have faced the harrowing storm of insolvency and its aftermath, who have watched as everything you built was taken from you—this book is for you.

For every director who has endured sleepless nights, personal sacrifices, and the painful fallout inflicted upon your families, know this: you did not deserve this.

You deserved a fair chance, a system that respected your courage and your efforts.

I am, and always will be, in your corner. I promise to fight for justice, for reform, and for the right of every entrepreneur to rise again.

You are not forgotten, and I will stand with you until my very last breath.

Patrick

Contents

Foreword 7
Introduction: 12
Champions of Innovation – Why We Must Celebrate and Protect Our Entrepreneurs 17
Limited Liability and the Vital Separation Between Director and Company 24
A History Lesson 32
The Rise and Misuse of the CVL 39
The Setup: How Accountants, Lawyers and IPs Collude to Trap Directors 48
Case Studies: Devastating CVLs 58
The Beast that Begbies Built: Systematic Manipulation 70
A System of Retribution, Not Re-education 79
The Fear Factor: Why Directors Won't Speak Out 88
What to Do with the Crooks? A New Approach to Investigations in Insolvency 97
The Insolvency Practitioners' Defence – A Narrative of Self-Preservation 109
The Economic Toll: How the Insolvency Industry is Killing Growth in the UK 118
The Personal Toll of Predatory Liquidations 126
A Global Comparison – How the Insolvency System in the UK Stacks Up Against the US and Europe 132
The Struggle for Reform and the Resistance to Change 140

Rethinking the Insolvency System for Small and Medium Businesses 147

Bloated Britian – The Other Factors 155

Reviving British Industry and Entrepreneurial Spirit 163

BonusDirector's Survival Guide 169

Foreword:

A Call to Defend the Heart of British Business

Nine years ago, I was the commercial manager of a thriving construction company, a seven-figure business that was rooted deeply in the local community. We didn't just build homes; we turned forgotten brownfield sites into places where families could actually live. It was a company that employed hundreds of local people—and I'd given everything to help build it. Two years earlier, my company had been bought out as a Groundworks Specialist, and I stayed on to steer the newly formed group commercially. The Group Director was a good family man who'd built the business from nothing.

Then the axe fell.

Our funding was tied to one private investor. He died in a freak accident, and suddenly his family were at each other's throats. Our funding froze. Our projects stalled. The lender—our main lender—held a first legal charge over everything, and it was going to take months to get it resolved. Cash flow severed. Projects left half-finished. And us, plunging into the abyss.

Accountants. Financial advisors. All the so-called "experts" that the director trusted were buzzing around him like vultures, telling him a CVL was the way forward. "It'll protect you," they said. It'll be "smooth", they said. Except it wasn't smooth. It was an execution. And these "experts". They weren't advisors; they were hitmen. They ripped through everything he had built—reduced it to rubble and ruin, all for a few hours' worth of billing. He didn't fail because he acted irresponsibly—he failed because he trusted a system that exists to devour rather than to help.

Watching that slow, inevitable collapse was my wake-up call. The UK's insolvency system didn't just f*ck over that director—it f*cked over every single employee, every local family who depended on his company. For what? For some petty satisfaction of "accountability", a pointless parade of "justice" where creditors still got zilch, zero, nada. The real winners? The insolvency practitioners, stuffing their pockets while they tore a man's life apart. This wasn't justice. This was *state-sanctioned annihilation* of a bloke who dared to try.

That was the moment everything changed for me. I couldn't just stand by and watch as this system ground another innocent director into the dirt. I founded a consultancy to help construction companies in distress—to avoid insolvency at all costs. But it didn't stop there. Directors from every kind of sector started coming to me, and that small consultancy grew into a firm that's helped over 1,000 companies battle through financial hell.

Since then, I've made it my mission to fight against this sickening system of predation. What started in construction is now a full-blown decade-long war against a machine designed to profit off human devastation.

The Red Flags: A System Fueled by Greed, Not Protection

I've seen it all. The lies, the tricks, the constant piling up of fees. Insolvency practitioners swear they're "protecting creditors," but it's bullshit. Creditors see pennies—if that. The real money? That's funding the IPs' Range Rovers, their London townhouses, their "business trips" to the Bahamas. They've taken what should be a crucial government duty—helping businesses survive—and turned it into a cash cow.

Real solutions? Forget it. Real interest in helping people? Laughable. They're here to fatten their wallets, and they'll keep doing it until someone stops them.

The UK's insolvency system is in desperate need of reform. Right now, it's a game rigged to destroy entrepreneurs who poured their lives into their companies—directors who made impossible choices and trusted in a process that repaid that trust with total obliteration. We need change—desperately. Directors should be educated, guided, not demonised and hung out to dry. Profit in insolvency? There should be none—zero—because it's a public responsibility, not some bloody racket.

If we let these IPs keep running their privatised empire unchecked, we're killing the spirit of British entrepreneurship. The risk-takers, the ones who create jobs, the innovators—they'll disappear. Drowned by a system that feeds on the very people who keep our economy breathing.

An Impassioned Plea

This book isn't just a rant—it's a call to arms. It's for every entrepreneur, policymaker, and citizen who believes in the potential of British business. I wrote it because directors deserve better than a system that chews them up for a quick buck. When businesses fail, there should be a way back—a way that doesn't destroy but instead rebuilds.

As you read, remember this: we're standing at a critical point. If we let this continue, if we keep letting the insolvency industry operate as a private hunting ground, we are surrendering the future of British entrepreneurship. But if we act—if we demand change—we can build a system that champions resilience, recovery, and real human grit.

This is your invitation to join the fight. The UK's entrepreneurs are the backbone of this country. They deserve a system that doesn't prey on them—one that stands by them. Let's tear down this predatory regime of private insolvency practitioners—for every director, every employee, every community that still dares to dream.

Introduction:

The Biggest Criminals of All

The UK has long been known as a place of opportunity, where anyone with a bit of grit and a decent idea can build something real. But for many British entrepreneurs, that promise has become nothing but an illusion—a trap set by a system just waiting for them to slip up. And right at the heart of this betrayal are the private insolvency practitioners (IPs), with far more power than they should ever have been trusted with. They don't just profit from tearing down struggling businesses—they chase directors long after the final nails are driven into the company's coffin, extinguishing any last spark of hope or ambition to rebuild.

This book is both a challenge to an industry and a warning to entrepreneurs. My name is Patrick Donnelly, and I've spent over a decade working with distressed companies across the UK. I've advised over 1,000 businesses through financial crises and the painful slog of corporate recovery. Nearly 400 of those were small, local businesses, with less than £250,000 in debt. For them, insolvency wasn't some cold boardroom decision—it was life or death. I've been on the phone with directors whose entire worlds have collapsed, talking them down from the brink of suicide. And sometimes, tragically, the line goes silent. These aren't just stories of business failure; they're stories of lives shattered by a system designed to profit from desperation.

A System That Punishes Ambition

It's one thing to liquidate a failing business—sometimes that's just how it goes. But what should come next is a chance for the entrepreneur to get back on their feet, reassess, and try again. If someone strays, the system should be a place of guidance, not a firing squad. But in the UK, that's a fantasy. Insolvency Practitioners don't let go—they hound directors long after their companies are dead, turning what should be a fresh start into a life sentence. They seize personal assets, brand directors as liabilities, and wring every ounce they can to recover debts. For most directors, it's such a traumatic experience that the idea of starting over is inconceivable. And that's the real tragedy.

The UK loses far more than individual businesses—it loses the creativity, resilience, and sheer bloody-mindedness of its entrepreneurs. These are the people who could be driving growth, creating jobs, building industries—if they were just given a fair shot. But instead, our country is suffocating under a culture of avoiding failure, perpetuated by IPs who profit when others fail. They don't just kill companies—they crush ambition, leaving the UK weaker, less inventive, and totally unprepared to compete globally.

My Journey: From Witness to Advocate

I'm not talking theory here. I've sat in the trenches with directors in their darkest moments, guiding them through a system designed to snuff out their dreams. I've been in boardrooms where millions were on the line, but I've also sat at kitchen tables with local business owners who were losing everything. For them, liquidation wasn't about salvaging an asset portfolio—it was about losing their family's income, their identity, their sense of worth.

Early in my career, I saw how the traditional insolvency process left directors broken—with no choices, no hope. I knew there had to be a better way—a way that gave people a fighting chance. So, I started carving out new paths for directors to manage their company's distress. I showed them how to negotiate directly with creditors, taking power away from the IPs. I introduced the idea of distressed sales and coached them on how to manage creditor negotiations themselves. This wasn't some miracle cure—but it put control back in their hands. And often, they walked away with their finances and dignity intact.

I've seen what happens when directors reclaim control. They go from being overwhelmed and powerless to confident and capable. Some managed to restructure and get back to profitability; others closed down with dignity, avoiding the financial ruin that IPs would have gladly overseen. In a system built to exploit distress, I've helped create real options for directors to find their footing again.

Why This Book?

The UK can't afford to lose its entrepreneurs to a system built to punish them for profit. We're facing an economic identity crisis, with fewer and fewer people willing to take the risks that drive growth and innovation. Over half a billion pounds in debt advised, and countless companies saved from the edge—I've seen what's possible when directors are given a real chance. This book exposes the truth about the insolvency industry: the conflicts of interest, the broken oversight, and the devastating human cost of a relentless, profit-driven pursuit.

But it's more than that. It's a vision for change—a call to build a system that values resilience over punishment, growth over loss. The solutions are there: empower directors with options, support them with genuine resources, create a framework where recovery is prioritised. With those changes, the UK could once again be a place where ambition is nurtured, where every entrepreneur has a shot at success, and even failure is just a step towards something better.

This book is a call to action. With a system that champions recovery and innovation, we can reignite the entrepreneurial spirit that has always been at the heart of British business. Together, we can create a landscape where our business owners aren't just shielded from exploitation—but empowered to build a future where success isn't just a fluke, but the result of courage, resilience, and the support of a fair and just system.

Champions of Innovation – Why We Must Celebrate and Protect Our Entrepreneurs

Entrepreneurs are more than just business owners—they are the brave (sometimes misguided) architects of change, the dreamers who see potential where everyone else just sees a terrible idea. They don't just work within systems; they dismantle them, hammer in some questionable additions, and pray the whole thing doesn't fall apart. Every time you pass a thriving business, step into a new restaurant, or use some ridiculous yet genius gadget, you're witnessing the sheer insanity of someone who decided to take a leap of faith—a big (occasionally outright stupid) risk. Let's be clear, entrepreneurship is not for the faint-hearted or the sane. It's a chaotic ride filled with highs, lows, and sudden cliff drops. These risk-takers aren't just adding jobs or boosting the economy; they're making communities better, investing in local suppliers, and creating spaces for people to gather and moan about their day.

And it's precisely because of this spirit of total madness that society should celebrate, protect, and support entrepreneurs—not only when they succeed but especially when they spectacularly fail.

In my own career, I've seen the resilience of entrepreneurs up close, particularly those who didn't have the luxury of a safety net. These are the people who put everything on the line—mortgages, marriages, sanity. And for what? To avoid ending up in Loserville, that bleak destination where everyone gets to say, "I told you so." Oh, and they will say it. Trust me.

Your sister-in-law, she never said it was obviously not going to work, she just hinted a little…

that maybe a restaurant needs parking nearby and, yes, although Cambridge suffers from a tragic shortage of Polynesian-themed Tapas Bars, it could possibly be because there is absolutely ZERO demand for one.

And your friend didn't outright tell you your new construction company was doomed, but he just voiced some concerns…

*that the construction industry runs on non-existent margins, with an aging, miserable workforce, in a country that rains 9/10 days and where 95% of companies go bust in less than a week. Oh, and everyone ends up an alcoholic, and your wife will leave with the kids—not because she doesn't love you anymore, but because it's "better for the kids to be away from the stress." And don't worry about Tony, he's just a friend but he **will** only be dropping the kids off every other Wednesday from now on…*

And yet, despite the almost absolute certainty of public humiliation, thousands of Brits still make the leap every single day. They walk away from their comfy 9-to-5s to do handstands on the edge of hellfire.

Good on them. Now, let's talk about why they really matter.

The Real Impact of Entrepreneurs: Building More Than Just Businesses

Entrepreneurs aren't just vital to economic growth—they're the pulse of their communities. They make things happen where nothing existed before, fill the gaps nobody else bothered with, and meet needs with a mix of wild passion and utter delusion. Think of the neighbourhood café that becomes a local hub, the grocer who stocks the good cheese that you can't find anywhere else, or the small construction company that helps rebuild after a storm. These businesses are not just money-making entities; they are part of the community's DNA, giving people a place to connect, complain, or just be.

These entrepreneurs bring real life to their communities. They create jobs, support local suppliers, and establish ecosystems that spark further growth. I've worked with hundreds of these individuals, some staring at the abyss, others dangling off the edge. And you know what? I've seen the incredible difference it makes when they get the chance to fight for their business rather than being shuffled along the path to insolvency like cattle to slaughter. It's these stories that keep my belief in entrepreneurs alive. They deserve a system that fights alongside them, not one that kicks them while they're down.

The Ripple Effect of Entrepreneurial Success

When entrepreneurs succeed, their success ripples far beyond the front door of their business. It reaches families, other businesses, the wider economy. Each thriving small business relies on a network of suppliers, service providers, and contractors who also benefit. And when that business does well, everyone it touches does well too. Money moves around locally, other businesses thrive, and the community starts to feel alive again. It's like a weird but wonderful chain reaction—all because someone decided to take an absurd risk.

Consider the family-run construction firm I once advised. They hit a rough patch—cash flow issues, market changes, the usual suspects. Instead of herding them towards the inevitable abyss of liquidation, we crafted a turnaround plan—restructure the debts, optimise the cash flow, re-engage the clients. Within a year, they were back, employing dozens of locals and contributing to the community. If they'd been pushed into insolvency, those jobs would have vanished, and a trusted business would have been erased. But we saw the potential, gave them the tools to claw back, and everyone won. Except maybe the insolvency practitioners, who I assume cried into their expensive whiskey that night.

Why We Need a System That Lets Entrepreneurs Bounce Back

Entrepreneurship is rarely a straight, smooth ride to glory. It's more like a poorly maintained rollercoaster—unpredictable, thrilling, with a high chance of derailing. The ones who make it aren't those who get it right every time, but those who learn from the crashes, dust themselves off, and keep going. And yet, our current system doesn't really allow for this kind of resilience. Too many directors, at the first sign of trouble, are nudged right over the edge into insolvency rather than being given a fighting chance to recover. It's sickening to see good businesses dismantled just because no one offered them a way out

There are so many ways to help businesses bounce back without defaulting straight to insolvency. I've helped companies negotiate directly with creditors, identify and fix cash flow issues, and restructure their operations to become profitable again. These approaches are less painful and more effective than insolvency—but they aren't offered nearly often enough. Instead, entrepreneurs are led down the garden path to liquidation, disqualification, or complete personal ruin. A system that doesn't value recovery doesn't value entrepreneurs—and that's got to change.

Repeat Entrepreneurs: A Unique Asset to the Economy

Some of the best entrepreneurs I've met are the ones who've failed, sometimes spectacularly, and come back for more. These are the folks who have tasted both the sweet highs of success and the bitter, often humiliating lows of failure. Repeat entrepreneurs are tougher, smarter, more resourceful – and crucially – more resilient. They know what works, what doesn't, and they've got the scars to prove it. They're less likely to make the same mistakes twice, and far more likely to build something meaningful and sustainable.

Imagine a business owner who's gone through hell—they've made the cuts, weathered the sleepless nights, fought tooth and nail to make it through. When they start over, they do it with knowledge, grit, and confidence that only experience can provide. They're more likely to mentor others, to share their hard-earned lessons, to give back. We should be celebrating this resilience, not punishing it. Repeat entrepreneurs are an asset we can't afford to squander. The ability to rise from failure should be a badge of honour, not a brand of shame.

A Call for a Safety Net, Not a Straightjacket

If we want entrepreneurs to keep pushing boundaries and innovating, we need a system that lets them take risks without fearing utter annihilation if things go sideways. I've worked with businesses where a minor slip spiralled into a near-death experience, but with the right help, they recovered and thrived. It's these cases that convince me—we need a proper safety net, a way to catch entrepreneurs when they fall and help them get back up.

Too often, entrepreneurs face unnecessary ruin because they're pushed into insolvency without fully understanding their options. These are people who could turn it around if given the right guidance—people who deserve better than being tossed aside. We need a system that supports entrepreneurs, educates them on recovery options, and gives them the breathing space to come back stronger. One that values education over punishment, support over disqualification, resilience over liquidation.

That's the fight I'm here for. And it's one hell of a fight worth having.

Limited Liability and the Vital Separation Between Director and Company

In the complex world of business, few principles are as foundational and essential as the concept of limited liability. This legal structure, which creates a clear distinction between a company and its directors, is the cornerstone of modern commerce. Limited liability allows individuals to engage in entrepreneurship without exposing their personal assets to the full financial risks of their business ventures. It's essentially the reason why, when your overly ambitious cousin from Burnley decides to start a company selling gourmet dog biscuits for vegan, yoga-practicing chihuahuas in the local area, they're not risking the family home. And thank god for that. *On second thoughts maybe he does deserve a bit of a kicking...*

Limited liability has shaped the economic landscape, enabled innovation, and given rise to a thriving culture of enterprise by ensuring that business owners, directors, and shareholders are legally distinct from the companies they create. This chapter dives into why this concept matters so much, how it came to be, and why the we need to protect it from outside profiteers who only have their short term interest in mind.

The Origins of Limited Liability: Why It Matters

Limited liability emerged as a way to convince people that, yes, you can take risks without ending up moving into your parents' back bedroom in your 40s, with your loving wife -

who will be absolutely thrilled at the prospect of sharing a toilet with her father-in-law. Back in the 1800s, when the industrial economy was booming, huge investments were needed to build factories and infrastructure. But without limited liability, people were understandably hesitant. I mean, who would be crazy enough to gamble everything—their savings, their spouse's savings, and the kids' wedding funds—on a business idea that might tank because a rival company invented a slightly better steam engine?

So in 1856, the UK passed the Joint Stock Companies Act, letting businesses be recognised as separate legal entities. This meant that if your ambitious venture went south, you wouldn't end up in debtor's prison (yes, that was a real thing). You'd just lose what you put in. It was like a magical forcefield that let people innovate, build, and create without worrying that a market downturn would mean they had to sell their bodies to the highest bidder on Victorian OnlyFans.

This principle remains the backbone of business today. It allows directors to do their job—which often involves making risky, forward-thinking decisions—without waking up at 3 AM in a cold sweat because some nutcase in South America invaded another nutcase in South America and what that will do to the July Futures price of soy beans. Limited liability encourages people to think big, take calculated risks, and make bold moves, knowing they're shielded from losing everything if things don't work out. In essence, it's what makes entrepreneurship as thrilling and as occasionally moronic as it is.

The Separation of Director and Company: More than a Legal Distinction

At its core, limited liability means that a company is its own person in the eyes of the law—though unlike people, a company can't eat, sleep, or complain about its mother-in-law. This "separate legal personality" means the company can enter contracts, own property, and, importantly, be sued—all without the director personally needing to stand in court biting their nails over whether they're going to lose the family car. Directors manage the company, but they do so on behalf of the company, not themselves personally. It's a well-designed law that lets you dream big without constantly fearing you're personally one bad decision away from losing it all.

In practical terms, this means if the company fails, the company goes bankrupt—not the director. The creditors can come for the company's assets, but they can't come for your home, your savings, or your future. This is especially important for small businesses, which often face enormous unpredictability. The safety net of limited liability allows them to keep innovating and pushing boundaries without the constant spectre of personal ruin hanging over their heads.

How Insolvency Practitioners Blur the Lines of Limited Liability

Now, in a perfect world, this principle would be rock-solid. Limited liability should mean what it says on the tin: the business fails, and the director's liability is limited. But that's where insolvency practitioners come swooping in, like vultures with second class law degrees from the Uni down the road that used to be a poly. *I'm sorry to get personal but they're just SO unimpressive.*

IPs often see limited liability less as a cornerstone of fair commerce and more as a grey area to exploit for their own benefit. Their goal? To blur the lines between what a company owes and what a director might have to cough up personally.

I've seen it countless times. An IP is appointed to deal with a struggling business, and suddenly the directors are being grilled about every coffee they ever expensed. The IP hints—subtly, of course—that there might be an issue with "preferential payments" or "questionable transactions," implying that the director could end up on the hook personally. It's classic scare tactics, and it works brilliantly because, well, no one wants to end up in court, especially if they don't fully understand what they're up against.

The goal is simple: scare the director enough that they'll do exactly what the IP says. Maybe it's agreeing to the initial Creditors' Voluntary Liquidation (CVL). Maybe it's rolling over and letting the IP milk every last drop of value from the company. In reality, most of these so-called "questionable transactions" amount to nothing. But the mere hint that personal finances might be dragged through the mud is usually enough to make directors comply—even when there's no real legal basis for it.

There'll be more on this later, don't worry.

The Broader Impact on the Business Environment

When IPs play these kinds of games, they don't just hurt individual directors. They erode trust across the whole system. Directors who've been burned like this often swear they'll never take a risk again, never build another company, never advise anyone to do so. It creates a chilling effect, like telling a kid the bogeyman will get them if they ever dare eat an extra cookie. The truth is, business is risky. Sometimes things fail. That's the nature of the game. But the threat of personal financial ruin where none should exist? That's not part of the game—that's just cheating.

And it's not just directors who lose out. Creditors lend money to companies with the understanding that, sure, it might not work out. They assess that risk. But when IPs start waving around the possibility of personal liability, it changes the terms entirely. Creditors didn't sign up for a situation where they'd be targeting someone's personal bank account, and it distorts the whole principle of commercial risk-taking.

The Slippery Slope: When Minor Errors Lead to Major Threats

The thing is, directors are human. They make mistakes. Sometimes they take cash from one account to cover another, or they pay a supplier early because they want to keep that relationship strong. Most of these decisions aren't made with malicious intent—they're just trying to keep the business afloat in a sea of chaos. Limited liability was designed to ensure that directors aren't personally destroyed for every minor slip-up unless there's clear evidence of fraud or gross negligence.

Yet IPs love to lean on these small mistakes. I once saw an IP go after a director for paying a critical supplier shortly before the business hit the rocks. The IP suggested this could be "preferential treatment," implying that the director could end up liable. This wasn't about justice; it was about using fear to get what they wanted. The director, terrified of losing their house, eventually rolled over and agreed to everything the IP asked. It was manipulation, pure and simple, and it completely disregarded the whole spirit of limited liability.

Again, more on this later...

Preserving Limited Liability: Why the Principle Must Be Respected

Limited liability is not just some bureaucratic detail. It's what lets people with good ideas but finite resources take a shot at building something amazing. If we allow IPs to keep muddying these waters, we're effectively saying that directors must face the risk of personal ruin every time they step up to the plate. Who would be ~~stupid~~ brave enough to take that deal?

For the business world to thrive, limited liability has to be respected by everyone involved—especially by those with the power to ruin lives. The line between what a company owes and what a director is personally responsible for must be upheld. Directors should be able to make bold decisions for the good of their companies without the threat that one wrong move could lead to losing their home. It's about fairness, about creating an environment that rewards effort, courage, and innovation, rather than punishing people for trying to do something valuable.

Defending a Critical Safeguard for Directors

Limited liability is what makes modern entrepreneurship possible. It's the shield that lets people take risks, build businesses, and drive the economy forward. When IPs mess with this principle for their own gain, they erode the very foundation that supports business innovation. They turn what should be an orderly process of managing business failure into a personal nightmare for directors, leaving them hesitant to ever try again.

To build a fairer system, we must respect the separation between a company and its directors. By defending limited liability, we ensure that entrepreneurship remains an accessible, viable path for those willing to take the plunge. Letting IPs blur this line not only hurts individuals but damages the entire ecosystem of growth and innovation that the UK so desperately needs. The principle is simple: take risks, innovate, and if it doesn't work out, the company fails—not the person behind it.

Leading into the History of Formal Insolvency

The need for a supportive, balanced approach to business failure is clear, but it's not something that's always been there. Formal insolvency has a long, complicated, and often brutal history in the UK, evolving from a way to handle debts fairly into something far more punitive. In the next chapter, we'll take a closer look at the history of insolvency and how, over time, private insolvency practitioners came to be – and how they became legalised robbers.

A History Lesson

Insolvency in the UK has a long and complex history, shaped by centuries of legislation, reform, and gradual privatisation. From its beginnings as a public concern managed by the Crown to its current form as a lucrative industry dominated by private practitioners, the journey of UK insolvency law has seen a noble cause, with the UK's ambitions and aspirations at its heart, slowly morph into a profit-hungry beast only concerned with self-preservation. What started off as a way to manage business failures in the public interest has become a system that puts IPs' profits front and centre, often at the cost of struggling directors and drained creditors.

This chapter is going to take you through this grim transformation—from a last-resort mechanism to a powerful industry built on fear, loopholes, and manipulation. I've been in the trenches, advising directors through crisis after crisis, and I have studied the history of corporate insolvency diligently - it's been like watching a benevolent doctor slowly turn into a deranged surgeon, all too happy to cut a little deeper because, hey, it pays well and who cares about the patient?

The Early Days: Crown-Controlled Insolvency (16th - 19th Centuries)

Back in the 16th century, insolvency wasn't seen as just a bad business outcome; it was seen as a moral failing, like stealing from the church or kicking your neighbour's dog. The Statute of Bankrupts of 1542 made sure of that. Insolvent debtors weren't just unlucky—they were criminals. You lost your business, your assets, and maybe your freedom. You got the distinct pleasure of being hauled off to a debtor's prison, where you could contemplate your crimes of not being able to magically make money appear. Lovely.

In those early days, insolvency was managed directly by the Crown. It wasn't a business, it was public service. Sheriffs would seize assets, pay creditors, and then go back to whatever other medieval duties they had—likely involving jousting or boiling someone who looked like a witch just for the craic. There was no profit motive. No one's eyes lit up at the thought of a debtor because, simply put, there wasn't any cash to be made. There was oversight, and there was no private practitioner turning the whole mess into a money-making scheme.

The Industrial Revolution and the Shift to Business Recovery (18th - 19th Centuries)

Then came the Industrial Revolution, a whirlwind of smoke, steam, and dodgy workplace safety. Bankruptcy became a lot more common. As the economy grew, the risks grew too. People began to realise that maybe—just maybe—bankruptcy wasn't always the result of moral failing. Maybe it had something to do with the cutthroat business environment or the sudden crash in coal prices because some nutcase in South America invaded his neighbour.

By the time we reached the Bankruptcy Act of 1825, there was a marked change in tone. Bankruptcy wasn't just about punishment anymore. It was about finding a way out, a fresh start—an idea that blew minds back then. Imagine being able to fail and not have to spend the rest of your life locked up for it! The Act of 1861 went even further and actually decriminalised bankruptcy, which was like telling everyone, "Hey, sometimes life screws you over, and that's okay." But insolvency was still managed by public officials, who worked with some basic sense of neutrality.

The Turn Toward Professionalisation (Late 19th - Early 20th Centuries)

Fast forward a few decades, and here comes the Bankruptcy Act of 1883, which introduced the Official Receiver. This was a government official whose job was to oversee bankruptcies fairly and responsibly—in theory, at least. The system still aimed to balance the interests of creditors and debtors. It wasn't perfect, but it was a damn sight better than what came next.

Then they let private trustees in. These guys were supposed to step in when the government didn't have the resources. It sounded reasonable enough, but we all know what happens when private interests come sniffing around public services. They set up camp, got cosy, and suddenly, the role of private trustees expanded. They started managing bigger cases, the ones with more money on the table, and before long, the idea of an impartial process started slipping out the back door.

The Rise of Privatised Insolvency: The Insolvency Act of 1986

The real kicker came in 1986 with the Insolvency Act. This Act opened the door wide open for private insolvency practitioners, letting them waltz in, take a seat, and then take over the whole table. Thatcher-era economic policies favoured deregulation and privatisation, and what better way to streamline insolvency than to let the 'experts' run the show? Whilst Thatcher in many ways saved the country – this is certainly one area where the result is only now coming home to roost. The idea was efficiency, but the reality was a loss of control. We'd moved from a system of public accountability to one where IPs could charge what they wanted, do as they pleased, and laugh all the way to the bank – regardless of the long term goals of Britain – I don't know, like not mercilessly beating every man or woman who dares to start a company.

From Public Service to Private Profit

I've studied insolvency laws change from a system designed to help failing businesses, or at least manage their closure fairly, into a cash cow for private practitioners. Today's IPs aren't neutral arbiters; they're businesspeople who have every incentive to milk cases for all they're worth. They prolong investigations, pile on the fees, and squeeze every last drop out of the business and, often, out of the directors. I had one director who thought the liquidation of their company would be straightforward. A year later, they were still dealing with "additional assessments" that seemed to have no purpose other than to line the IP's pockets.

The Modern Landscape: Privatisation Gone Wild

Today, the UK insolvency landscape is basically privatisation on steroids. Nearly all cases are handled by private IPs, and the Official Receiver has been sidelined to a minor role— even cases that enter a Compulsory Liquidation are now being handed off to private practitioners. These IPs are now largely self-regulated, and let's be honest, self-regulation works about as well as putting the fox in charge of the henhouse. *I'm not sure I even blame them for what they do… no, I do, it's evil. Sorry.*

IPs have become gatekeepers of business failure, armed with the power to scrutinise, dismantle, and personally pursue directors whenever they see fit—usually, when they see a chance to make an extra buck.

Take retrospective scrutiny, for instance. I've seen directors face relentless questioning about financial decisions that were perfectly reasonable when they made them. But years later, an IP decides that these decisions look "suspicious," mainly because there's money to be clawed back. One client was asked to personally repay company expenses that were entirely legitimate at the time, but which the IP decided were "questionable"—conveniently adding to their billable hours.

The System Today: A Profit Machine at the Expense of British Business

The UK insolvency system today is a profit machine where IPs hold all the cards. Directors, who should be learning from failure and rebuilding, are left in a system that profits from their misery. Creditors, who think they're going to be repaid, end up with scraps while the IPs take the lion's share. And the wider economy loses out because the entrepreneurial spirit is being systematically crushed by the fear that one slip-up means financial ruin, public shaming, and a drawn-out ordeal with an IP who's financially motivated to keep digging.

I've seen directors broken by this process, their dreams turned to dust by a system that's supposed to help. The UK needs an insolvency system that genuinely supports failing businesses and allows directors to bounce back. Instead, we have one that preys on failure, rewarding IPs for prolonging misery and monetising mistakes. In the chapters ahead, I'll take you deeper into this dysfunctional industry, show you exactly how IPs profit from business failure, and what needs to change to give directors a fair shot at recovery.

If we want innovation, if we want businesses to thrive, then we need an insolvency system that supports risk-takers, not one that gleefully punishes them. Right now, the UK's system is broken—and it's about time we fixed it.

Up next, the most trusty steed of the 80 IQ IP – the CVL.

The Rise and Misuse of the CVL

The Creditors' Voluntary Liquidation (CVL) was supposed to be an orderly, dignified exit—a final bow for companies that couldn't keep juggling their financial obligations. In theory, it's a way for insolvent companies to go quietly into the night without the pandemonium of a forced liquidation, making sure everyone involved—directors, creditors, employees—gets treated with some respect. But let's not kid ourselves. In practice, the CVL has become the favourite plaything of insolvency practitioners (IPs), who milk it like a cash cow at the expense of everyone else. Over the past 25 years, the CVL has morphed from a last-resort solution into the go-to recommendation, the default sledgehammer for every corporate headache—one that just so happens to be conveniently profitable for the IPs wielding it.

What a CVL Should Be: The Ideal Process

The CVL process was formalised under the Insolvency Act of 1986, which was meant to modernise the UK's approach to business failure. Here's how it's supposed to work:

1. **Initiation by the Directors**: When directors realise the company can't pay its bills, they should have the chance to start a CVL, acting responsibly to close the company in a way that limits damage. The whole idea is that they can take proactive steps to stop the bleeding without making a mess of it.

2. **Appointment of an Insolvency Practitioner (IP)**: Directors pick an IP who is supposed to guide the company through the liquidation. In an ideal world,

this IP is like a neutral referee, ensuring fairness for everyone involved.

3. **Approval by Shareholders and Creditors**: The IP arranges meetings where shareholders and creditors give the go-ahead for liquidation. Shareholders agree to close up shop, and creditors get their say on how it's done. It's supposed to be democratic, giving creditors a fair voice.

4. **Asset Liquidation and Debt Settlement**: The IP sells off company assets to pay the creditors. There's an order to things—secured creditors and employees are supposed to get paid first. The IP's job is to make sure this happens smoothly, with as much transparency as possible.

5. **Final Reporting and Closure**: Once everything is wrapped up, the IP files the paperwork, and the company is dissolved. The directors get to walk away knowing they've handled things responsibly. Ideally, everyone can move on, lessons learned, ready to face the world again.

The Abuse of the CVL Process by IPs

But that's the fairytale version. In reality, each stage of the CVL has been twisted into an opportunity for IPs to make a buck, and a big one at that. Let's break down the real-life scam that is the modern CVL.

1. **Initiation by the Directors: Manipulation from the Start**

IPs have become experts at selling the CVL as the only option, pushing it as the "quick and clean" fix. Forget about restructuring or any sort of creative solution that might actually save the business—those don't pay as well. Directors, already overwhelmed, get nudged into a CVL with promises of simplicity and safety, without being properly informed about the personal ramifications or the alternatives. It's a setup from the word go.

2. **Appointment of an IP: Conflict of Interest**

Once appointed, the IP gains control over everything—the assets, the operations, the books. Theoretically, they're there to be impartial, but that's a joke. The longer the process, the more complicated it gets, the higher their fees. Of course they're going to suggest a "thorough" investigation or a needlessly extended asset sale. They've got bills to pay too—theirs, not the company's.

3. **Approval by Shareholders and Creditors: Limited Transparency**

When creditors get involved, it's usually nothing but a box-ticking exercise. They receive just enough information to stay confused and compliant, and any concerns they raise are casually brushed aside. Most of them end up nodding along because the IP has all the cards and knows how to play them. Meanwhile, the IP prepares to siphon off funds while creditors hope—usually in vain—for a decent return.

4. **Asset Liquidation and Debt Settlement: A Slow Bleed**

This is where IPs really cash in. Every asset is another payday. "Assessing value" takes forever. Negotiating sales? Even longer. The process drags on, conveniently padding the billable hours until the remaining value has all but evaporated. By the time everyone else gets paid, there's almost nothing left. This isn't liquidation to recover value; it's liquidation to systematically extract fees.

5. **Investigation of Directors and Clawback Attempts: Retrospective Exploitation**

Then comes the clawback. The IP combs through years of company records, not so much looking for real misconduct as much as anything that could be twisted into an excuse to demand more money. Transactions that were perfectly above board become questionable in hindsight, because—surprise, surprise—there's profit in it for the IP. Directors, already under pressure, are hit with threats of personal liability for actions they took in good faith. It's not about justice. It's about creating more opportunities for fees.

6. **Final Reporting and Closure: Delays for Profit**

Even at the supposed end, IPs like to drag their feet. "Unresolved issues" or "ongoing investigations" provide convenient excuses to keep the company in limbo and keep the fees rolling in. Directors can be left in financial purgatory for months, sometimes years, with no ability to move forward or rebuild—all because their IP can't seem to file the final papers.

The Surge in CVL Use Over the Past 25 Years

The numbers tell the story. In 1997, there were about 4,800 CVLs. By 2022, that number had jumped to over 12,800. Back in the late '90s, CVLs were about 45% of corporate insolvencies. Today? Over 70%. Sure, the 2008 crash and the COVID pandemic played a role, but let's be honest—those figures represent more than just tough economic conditions. This is an industry shift, pure and simple. IPs have decided that CVLs are the quickest, easiest way to make the most money, and they're pushing them at every turn.

Why CVLs Are So Profitable for Insolvency Practitioners

The CVL process is a cash grab for IPs, who profit in multiple ways:

1. **Initial Setup Fees**: The initial consultation and creditor notification costs can rack up tens of thousands, and that's just the beginning.

2. **Ongoing Liquidation Fees**: Every step of liquidation—valuing, assessing, selling—is an opportunity to add more billable hours. The more "complex" the process, the more they make.

3. **Investigation and Clawback Fees**: IPs love a good investigation. They get to bill for every hour spent sifting through old records, writing threatening letters, and dragging directors through pointless legal hurdles.

Impact on Directors, Creditors, and Employees

Directors: They're the most obvious targets. IPs use retrospective scrutiny to intimidate them, questioning legitimate decisions and demanding personal repayments. Directors who went into the CVL expecting closure instead end up financially crippled.

Creditors: Despite the lip service paid to protecting creditor interests, most end up with peanuts. After IPs finish charging their fees, unsecured creditors are lucky to get 4% of what they're owed. It's a farce.

Employees: They're collateral damage. Redundant, left out in the cold, and with no say in the process. Their livelihoods are sacrificed for a process designed to ensure the IPs come out on top.

The Financial Toll of CVLs on the Broader Economy

Each CVL doesn't just kill a company—it disrupts entire supply chains, destroys jobs, and discourages potential entrepreneurs. The broader economy bleeds value to the tune of an estimated £4 billion annually in lost opportunities and stunted growth. When a business is forced into liquidation, it's not just the direct employees and creditors who suffer—it sends ripples throughout the entire network of suppliers, subcontractors, and even customers. A single company going under can mean a supplier loses a major client, forcing them to cut jobs or, worse, face insolvency themselves.

Local economies are hit especially hard. Imagine a small manufacturing company in a town where employment opportunities are already scarce. When that business goes into a CVL – unnecessarily - the economic impact isn't just numbers on a spreadsheet. Jobs are lost, consumer spending drops, and the community's economic heartbeat takes a significant hit. Shops see fewer customers, local services go underutilised, and the whole area starts to feel the drag of one company's demise.

Moreover, the chilling effect on entrepreneurship is very real. The idea of starting a business should be invigorating, an exciting leap into innovation and opportunity. Instead, would-be entrepreneurs look at this predatory insolvency landscape and think twice. The risk isn't just about whether their idea will succeed—it's the knowledge that if things go wrong, they'll be at the mercy of a system that prioritises extracting every last penny over any fair or dignified resolution. The prospect of seeing everything they worked for getting devoured by IP fees, with nothing left for creditors or themselves, is enough to deter even the most determined founders.

The broader economy also loses out on the innovation these entrepreneurs could bring. Every business that isn't started, every idea that doesn't get funded because of fear of the IP-dominated insolvency machine, is a missed opportunity for growth and progress. Instead of fostering a culture of resilience, where failing businesses can close responsibly and leave room for new ventures, we have an environment where failure is tantamount to economic execution—swift, ruthless, and with no chance of redemption.

The result? A stagnant economic atmosphere where people play it safe. Established businesses hesitate to take risks that could propel growth, fearing the consequences if it doesn't pan out. Potential new players decide to keep their savings in the bank rather than risk creating something new, knowing that if they fail, the CVL process will chew them up and spit them out, leaving nothing but scraps for everyone else. The UK economy loses its dynamism, its entrepreneurial drive, and its edge—all because the system that should support recovery has been turned into a profitable weapon for IPs.

CVLs as a Misused Tool for Profit

CVLs have transformed from a desperate last resort into an overused, profit-driven default. It's a symptom of an industry that's turned the misfortune of business failure into a lucrative game—one that prioritises private gain over public good. CVLs should offer a responsible way for companies to bow out, but instead, they've become the IP's cash register.

In the next chapter, we'll dive deeper into the conflicts of interest that plague the IP industry, showing exactly how they've engineered the CVL to suit their own ends. Spoiler alert: it's not pretty, but it's time someone shone a light on this dark corner of UK business.

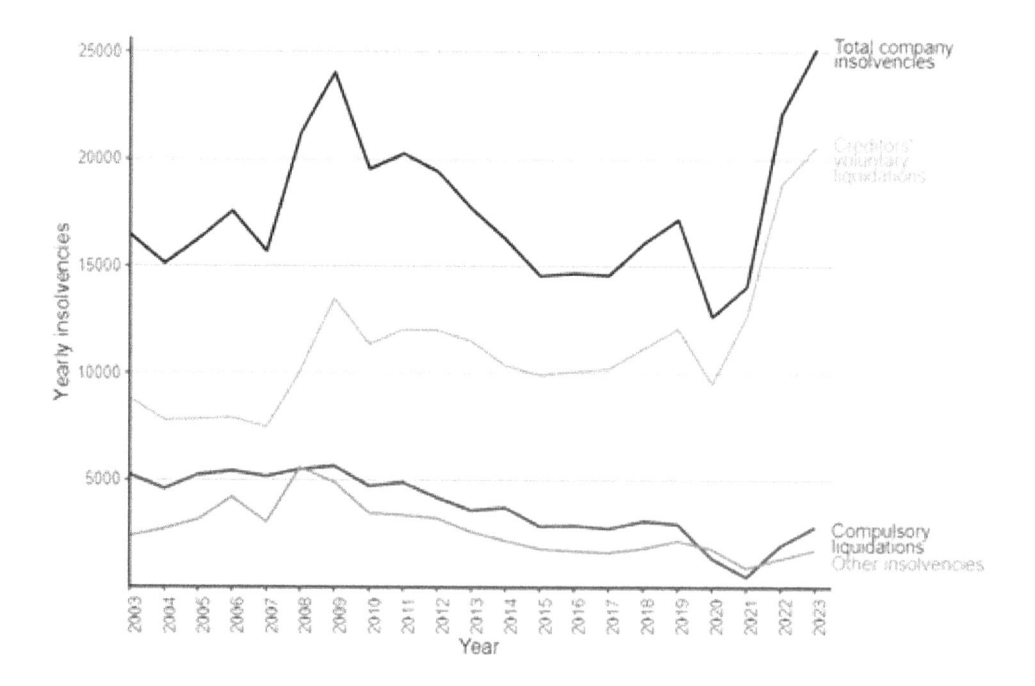

FIGURE 1 – 7,000 CVLs in 2003 to 20,577 in 2023

Source: The Insolvency Service/Companies House

The Setup: How Accountants, Lawyers and IPs Collude to Trap Directors

In today's UK, a vast cartel of accountants, lawyers, and policymakers operates in perfect harmony with insolvency practitioners (IPs)—a stitched-together Frankenstein designed to siphon struggling businesses into the abyss. What looks like a complex network is actually straightforward: ensure a steady flow of failing companies and milk them dry while the directors, creditors, and employees are left in the rubble. Originally created to help smooth over the ugly bits of business failure, the insolvency system has turned into a ravenous beast—one where everyone who touches it profits, except for those in actual distress.

This chapter will expose how accountants, lawyers, and lawmakers work tirelessly to keep the gears greased, maintaining a system where IPs thrive while businesses collapse. It's collusion, plain and simple. This isn't some inevitable business cycle—it's a business model.

Accountants: The First Line of Control

Accountants are often the first ones called when a business starts to nosedive. Directors turn to them, not just for numbers, but for advice—hoping to get a rope, a lifeline, something to pull them back from the edge. What they get instead is often a shove. Behind the concerned facade, many accountants are financially tied to the IP industry. Exclusive partnerships, kickbacks, referral fees—it's all part of the same game.

For accountants, handing over a struggling client to an IP isn't just a convenient option; it's lucrative. Referral fees can range from a few hundred pounds to a small percentage of the insolvency bill itself. In practice, this turns accountants into glorified scouts for the insolvency industry. I've seen directors who went to their accountant looking for breathing room and walked away with a liquidation order they never wanted. Honest advice? Not when there's a big payout at the end of the referral chain.

The web of referrals is spun in the shadows—accountants, who are supposed to be trusted advisors, end up being the gatekeepers into insolvency hell. Directors are led down the path under the guise of "professional guidance," not knowing they're just pawns in someone else's money-making scheme. In one case I advised, a director found himself referred to an IP within hours of asking for debt advice. There was no effort, no creativity, just an accountant sniffing the opportunity to cash in. It's more than negligent; it's predatory.

The Setup: Referrals in One Direction

Accountants are the first point of contact for many struggling directors—supposedly trusted advisors in times of trouble. But what most directors don't realise is that the game is rigged from the moment they reach out for help. These referrals are not about finding the best path for a struggling business; they're about feeding the insolvency pipeline. Once a director utters the word "trouble" in the presence of one of these accountants, they've triggered a sequence that leads straight to liquidation, with hardly a fork in the road.

Referral fees, kickbacks, preferred provider arrangements—call them what you like, they all lead in one direction. It's as if there's a one-way sign hanging over the doorway between the accountant's office and the IP's boardroom. And the way these referrals are framed to directors makes it all seem perfectly logical and inevitable. It's never, "Maybe you could talk to an IP to explore a few options." No, it's always, "You need an insolvency practitioner. Now." The accountants don't suggest alternative strategies, and why would they? There's no payout for recommending a financial restructure that could save the business but cut out the IP entirely.

The very nature of these arrangements ensures that when a company shows signs of distress, the accountant isn't looking for creative ways to save it. They're looking for a signpost that points straight to their favoured IP. They act like ambulance chasers in suits, more interested in their cut of the liquidation pie than in what's best for their clients. For the director, it's a betrayal of the highest order. They walked in expecting a lifeline and were instead handed a shovel and told to start digging.

The Referral Playbook

In practice, this is how it works: the moment an accountant spots the tell-tale signs of distress—missed payments, a wobbly cash flow, creditors beginning to circle—they play their part in the referral game. A call is made, a meeting is set up, and within days, the director finds themselves in a conference room with an insolvency practitioner, who wastes no time in explaining why liquidation is the "cleanest and safest route." There's no mention of restructuring or negotiation with creditors—just a fast dive into the abyss.

Directors don't know they're being played. They don't see the backroom deals, the lunches, the quid-pro-quo arrangements that grease the wheels of these referrals. They're just desperate for a solution. And accountants, with their cool demeanours and jargon-laced explanations, nudge them precisely where they want them to go: directly into the jaws of the IP who's ready and waiting. It's a seamless handoff—like a finely-tuned production line. Each player knows their role, and each step has been rehearsed countless times before.

The accountants' office is merely the entryway. Once they've handed the case off, they're paid for their loyalty, their pockets lined by the very practitioners they're supposed to remain impartial from. The more they feed into the insolvency system, the more they stand to gain. It's no coincidence that when the chips are down, so few directors are told about their real options. They're not warned that a CVL will likely leave creditors out in the cold or that liquidation means their employees will be given their marching orders overnight. No, those inconvenient truths are glossed over in favour of the grand narrative—crafted to seem inevitable—that liquidation is the only answer.

Statistics on Referral Trends

In the UK, more than 50% of insolvency cases begin with accountant referrals. Of these, a staggering majority are immediately pushed into CVLs—no restructuring, no renegotiation, just a straight-line descent. According to the Institute of Chartered Accountants, nearly 65% of distressed businesses are passed off to IPs within 60 days of a problem arising, like a hot potato no one wants to deal with. It's less about exploring options and more about closing the trapdoor.

The Influence of 'Preferred Provider' Arrangements

A lot of these referrals come through so-called 'preferred provider' arrangements. On the surface, they sound innocent—streamlined help, right? But these cozy deals ensure that once a business enters the orbit of insolvency, it has almost no chance of escape. Accountants get their cut, IPs get the case, and directors? They get destroyed, all while this scheme continues masquerading as "professional advice."

Lawyers: The Enforcers

If accountants are the gatekeepers, lawyers are the ones who slam the door shut. Once the IP takes over, the lawyers come marching in—drafting documents, issuing threats, clawing back anything they can find. It's not about justice, and it's certainly not about helping anyone other than themselves. Many law firms have built their entire practice on insolvency, thriving on the steady stream of liquidations, which, not coincidentally, they help keep flowing.

For these lawyers, a CVL is a blank cheque. Demand letters, endless litigation, chasing directors for anything they might have taken out of the company—all of it is billed, and all of it piles onto the mess. IPs need aggressive legal partners, and lawyers need the steady work that insolvency brings. It's symbiosis—each side benefits, and the debtor pays the price.

Cost Analysis of Legal Fees in CVLs

Legal fees now gobble up an average of 20% of a CVL's total costs. In the last decade, this figure has jumped by 30%, and in some high-profile cases, it's as high as 40%. I've seen companies bleed out, their remaining value lost not to creditors but to lawyers pushing paper. This isn't just about justice; it's about getting paid. And each legal step, no matter how pointless, serves to enrich those on the periphery.

Policymakers: The Puppet Masters

Behind the accountants and lawyers are the policymakers—faceless, nameless, working behind closed doors to keep the IP industry on a fast track to profit. They write the rules, grant the powers, and then look the other way. Their legislative work has built a system where IPs can operate with virtually unchecked power, exploiting directors who've already been kicked to the ground. Lobbying efforts from the insolvency industry make sure of it.

R3, the Association of Business Recovery Professionals, is the voice of the IP lobby. It claims to represent "business recovery" but spends most of its time ensuring IPs can continue charging unregulated fees. In 2015, when the government floated the idea of capping IP fees, R3's lobbying machine went into overdrive, claiming caps would "hurt creditors' chances of recovery." The proposal was gutted.

Since then, IP fees have soared, the only thing being recovered being the IP's profit margins.

Case Study in Lobbying Influence

Look at what happened in 2015. The government tried—briefly—to cap IP fees. R3 and their cohort bombarded them with propaganda about how it would hurt creditors. In reality, it would have hurt the IPs' bottom line, and that was enough for the proposal to be killed. What's left is a landscape where IPs can set their own rules, run their own show, and leave destruction in their wake.

A Self-Sustaining Profit Model

The collusion between accountants, lawyers, and IPs forms a cycle—a feeding frenzy where everyone but the struggling business gets paid. Accountants scout for clients, IPs run the liquidation, and lawyers extract every last penny, all while policymakers ensure nothing changes. Directors trust their accountants, who push them towards insolvency, and the IPs take over. It's like handing over the keys to your home, only for it to be gutted while you're forced to watch from the street.

Impact on the Broader Economy

It's not just individual directors who are hurt. The broader impact on the economy is severe—this hostile insolvency environment discourages risk-taking, stifles innovation, and slows growth. Why would you put your neck on the line if you know the system is rigged to kick you when you're down? In countries with recovery-focused systems like Germany, over 60% of businesses manage to restructure and survive. In the UK, that number is less than 15%. Here, liquidation is the first and last word, and it's killing entrepreneurship.

The Need for Transparency and Reform

This is not how insolvency was meant to work. If the system is to regain any legitimacy, it needs transparency—accountants should disclose referral kickbacks, IPs should cap their fees, and the cozy relationships must be brought into the light. Directors deserve a fighting chance, creditors deserve a real recovery, and employees deserve more than to be the collateral damage in this profit-driven system.

We don't need to tear it all down; we just need it to work for everyone, not just the suits making the referrals. Transparency, accountability, and oversight could turn this from a vulture's feast into something that actually serves those in need.

More on this later…

Exposing the Rigged System

The insolvency industry operates like a well-oiled machine, with each cog turning in sync—accountants, lawyers, policymakers, IPs—all part of the same monstrous system. And for anyone caught in it, the outcome is almost always the same: they lose everything while everyone else gets paid. It's a game that no one except the insiders knows how to win.

In the next chapter, we'll pull back the curtain even further—diving into a case study of one prominent insolvency firm to reveal exactly how they use their position in this ecosystem to their advantage, at the expense of the struggling businesses they're supposedly there to save.

Case Studies: Devastating CVLs

In late 2021, I was contacted by the director of a mid-sized manufacturing business that had just been forced into liquidation. The company, which employed close to 100 people, was in the hands of an insolvency practitioner (IP) who, rather than working to save the business, appeared to be on a mission to maximise fees at the expense of everyone involved. By the time I was called in, it was too late to reverse the process; the company had initially entered administration, only to be swiftly pushed into a Creditors' Voluntary Liquidation (CVL). What should have been a responsible approach to restructuring quickly became a destructive liquidation, with far-reaching consequences for employees, creditors, and the community.

This case shows just how damaging the CVL process can become in the hands of a profit-driven IP. There was no genuine attempt to save the business, no exploration of recovery options, and no thought for the people affected. It was a textbook example of how the current system can fail—and even devastate—those it was meant to protect.

The Company: A Family Business with Community Roots

This wasn't some faceless corporate giant. It was a family-run manufacturing business that had been part of the community for decades. Close to 100 employees. Deep community ties. They weren't just making products—they were providing livelihoods, putting food on the table for local families, building a reputation for high-quality craftsmanship. When the financial crisis hit, thanks to supply chain disruptions and sector slowdowns, the director did what anyone would do—he sought advice. He went to an accountant who, instead of working on internal solutions, sent him straight to an insolvency practitioner. The accountant said the IP would "handle everything" and that administration was just a "temporary fix." Trusting this advice, the director walked into what he thought was a safety net. In reality, it was a spider's web.

The Insolvency Practitioner's Role: From Administration to CVL in Record Time

The IP wasted no time. The company entered administration with hopes of restructuring, of buying time to salvage contracts, stabilise cash flow, and re-engage with creditors. Instead, within weeks, the IP declared that administration was "unviable." No real discussion. No thorough exploration of alternatives. Just the quick announcement that the only way forward was to go into a CVL. The director—who had started this journey looking for a way to save his company—found himself completely sidelined. The IP was on a mission, and that mission was liquidation, as fast as possible.

Initial Fees and the Transition to CVL: Profiting from Every Step

The fees started piling up from day one. Over £60,000 in "setup fees" for administration—paperwork, consultations, asset valuations—and before anyone could even catch their breath, the company was being ushered into CVL, with the IP insisting that "a different approach" was required. The "different approach" meant a new avalanche of fees—new valuations, new creditor correspondence, fresh investigations. By the time the CVL was in full swing, the total fees had hit £150,000, draining almost every remaining asset before any creditor saw a penny.

Asset Stripping: Rapid Liquidation with Minimal Returns

The liquidation itself was a fire sale. Equipment valued at over £1 million sold off in a rushed auction for less than £250,000. Machinery that had been essential to production was auctioned off at bargain-basement prices, sometimes to buyers who clearly knew they were getting a steal. There was one local entrepreneur who wanted to buy a big chunk of the equipment, even proposing to keep some employees on board for a gradual wind-down. But his offer was shot down by the IP due to supposed "administrative complexities." Instead, bespoke machinery that had been valued at £60,000 went for a pathetic £5,000. The whole liquidation brought in barely £250,000—a fraction of the company's worth—but enough to ensure the IP's fees were covered. Everyone else? Out of luck.

Employees: Overlooked and Disregarded

Nearly 100 employees were left out in the cold. Many had spent years—decades—working for this business. It was their source of stability, their pride. When the CVL was pushed through, they got termination notices and minimal redundancy payments through a government scheme. Employees who'd dedicated half their lives to the company were left with nothing. One worker, who had been there for 20 years, said she felt "discarded like yesterday's rubbish." The sudden closure left them reeling, struggling to find work in a sector that offered little hope. The director, who had always seen his employees as extended family, was shattered. He had imagined a gradual, respecttful wind-down—what they got was a hatchet job.

Creditors: Promises Broken, Returns Decimated

The IP's lip service to creditors was almost comical in its cynicism. "Every effort is being made to maximise value," they said. But when the dust settled, and the IP had taken their cut, the creditors were left with next to nothing. Some got as little as 1% of what they were owed. A major supplier, owed over £200,000, received a cheque for just £3,000—an insult. "I'd have been better off walking away from the start," he told me. Another creditor, who had extended a loan to help the business expand, got £1,500 out of a £50,000 debt. This was a financial massacre, orchestrated by the very people who were supposed to protect the process.

The Director: Financially Ruined and Emotionally Broken

The director went into the process trusting the system—trusting that administration would give him the breathing room to save his company. Instead, he found himself financially ruined. Every transaction, every decision of the past five years, was put under the microscope by the IP, desperate to find anything "questionable" they could use to squeeze more money out of him. Personal repayments were demanded on what the IP deemed "suspicious expenses"—in reality, these were just standard operational costs, twisted into something nefarious to justify more fees. By the end, his personal savings were gone, eaten up by legal battles and IP demands. He was left with nothing but bitterness—betrayed by a system that pretended to offer help.

A System That Failed Everyone—Except the Insolvency Practitioner

This wasn't just a business failure; it was a systemic failure. The employees, the creditors, the director—all were left in the rubble, while the IP walked away with hundreds of thousands of pounds in fees. The company had potential. With genuine restructuring, it could have survived, saved jobs, preserved value. Instead, the IP chose the quick and profitable route: liquidation, asset-stripping, fee extraction—leaving nothing but devastation in their wake.

The Family-Run Retail Outfit: A Struggle Turned Into Catastrophe

In 2022, Sarah and her husband, Mark, owned and operated a family-run retail shop that had been part of their local community for over 30 years. They sold clothing and accessories, providing a carefully chosen selection that was unique to their local high street. The business was not just a source of income; it was an integral part of their identity. They had regular customers, many of whom had been coming for years, and they prided themselves on offering personalized service that the larger chain stores could not replicate.

However, after COVID-19 and subsequent lockdowns, foot traffic plummeted, and revenues fell sharply. Sarah and Mark explored various ways to keep the store running: they adapted by setting up an online shop, but with competition from larger retailers, profits barely covered the costs of staying afloat. When they approached their accountant, they were told that insolvency was the only realistic path forward.

This advice came without any mention of other potential recovery options, such as negotiating with landlords or suppliers for extended terms.

Their accountant referred them to an insolvency practitioner, who initiated a CVL. Within weeks, their hopes for restructuring were dashed. The practitioner assured them that liquidation would be the cleanest way to proceed, stressing that attempting to save the business could put their personal assets at risk.

Liquidation and Its Aftermath

The IP moved quickly, with initial fees totaling over £25,000, covering administration and "asset valuations." Mark watched as their shop inventory, which had been carefully sourced and selected over decades, was sold off in a hurried auction for a mere fraction of its value. Shelves filled with unique items that had represented their life's work were emptied in a matter of hours. They saw stock worth over £200,000 go for less than £25,000 in total, leaving them devastated.

The emotional impact was equally severe. Mark, who had grown up helping his parents run the shop before taking it over himself, found himself dealing with sleepless nights, anxiety, and an overwhelming sense of failure. Their customers, many of whom they considered friends, were left stunned when the store closed without warning. One of their most loyal customers even sent them a letter, saying that it felt as if the heart had been ripped out of the community.

The IP's final fees ended up exhausting almost all the funds from the sale of assets, leaving little for creditors and nothing for Sarah and Mark. Today, they are working minimum wage jobs, trying to recover, but they have lost their home and face an uncertain financial future. For them, the insolvency process wasn't a way to manage business debt—it was a fast-track to personal disaster.

The impact on the community was just as devastating. Their shop had been a staple of the high street—a place where locals would come not just to buy clothing but to chat, share stories, and build connections. When the store disappeared, it left a void. Long-time customers who depended on Sarah and Mark for their carefully curated, personal touch now had to turn to faceless online giants or large chain stores that offered no sense of community. It wasn't just a loss for Sarah and Mark; it was a loss for the whole high street.

Even their suppliers suffered. They had long-established relationships with small designers and manufacturers who relied on regular orders to keep their own businesses afloat. When the store went under, these suppliers lost a major outlet for their products. A local jewellery maker, who had depended on Sarah and Mark's store to showcase her work, was left scrambling for new opportunities. She told me, "It wasn't just their dream that ended. It was a part of mine too."

And what of Sarah and Mark's personal toll? They had their entire lives tied up in that shop. Their children had grown up there, playing behind the counter and learning the value of hard work. They had poured their souls into every display, every product choice, every customer interaction. Losing it wasn't just financial—it was deeply personal. The anxiety and the sleepless nights that followed were relentless. They went from being respected business owners to feeling like failures, stripped of their dignity and self-worth. The IP's promise of a clean exit had been nothing but a cruel illusion.

The Tech Startup: The Innovator's Dream Turned Nightmare

Alex started a tech company in 2019, developing software to help small businesses manage supply chains. It was innovative, promising, and by early 2021, they were close to securing a major partnership that could change the game. But when their primary investor pulled out, the cash flow collapsed. Desperate, Alex sought advice from a financial advisor, who conveniently had a referral deal with an IP. Within a week, Alex was being pushed into a CVL, with assurances that their technology would be sold and their employees looked after.

The Collapse

It was all lies. The IP sold the company's intellectual property within two weeks to a buyer linked to the IP—and for a price far below market value. The software Alex had poured their life into was now being repurposed and sold by a competitor. The employees were unceremoniously dumped. Sam, one of the team members who had moved across the country for this job, found himself jobless, facing mounting bills, and waiting months for statutory redundancy payments. Alex? They were left broke and broken. The technology they'd nurtured was now generating profit for someone else, while they struggled to make ends meet. It was a betrayal by a system that claimed to help but was only there to profit.

The psychological toll on Alex was profound. Entrepreneurship had been his dream, and he had genuinely believed that the software could change the game for small businesses. It wasn't just about profit—it was about empowerment, about giving smaller players a fighting chance in a market dominated by big corporations. The collapse of his startup wasn't just the loss of a business; it was the death of that vision. Watching the software he had nurtured repackaged and sold by a competitor, while he struggled to make rent, was a gut punch that left him reeling.

The way the IP handled the liquidation was a textbook case of negligence and conflict of interest. Selling to a buyer linked to the IP at a knockdown price wasn't just unethical—it was predatory. And what about the employees? Many of them had left stable jobs, uprooted their lives to be part of something they believed in. Sam, who had moved across the country, ended up living in his car for three weeks after losing his job. The redundancy payments took so long to arrive that by the time they did, they barely made a dent in the debt he'd accumulated just trying to survive.

Alex now struggles with trust issues, not just with financial advisors and IPs, but with the entire system. He wonders if he'll ever be able to put his faith in anything like that again. The sense of betrayal is overwhelming—his dream turned into someone else's profit, and the people who were supposed to guide him through a tough time had been there only to exploit him. It's the kind of experience that kills not just a business, but the entrepreneurial spirit itself.

The Construction Company Collapse

John ran a small building firm that focused on local housing projects. He employed around 15 people, mostly tradespeople, who relied on the work for their livelihood. The company had managed well through the ups and downs of the industry, but rising material costs and a delay in a significant payment from a contractor put John in a difficult position. John approached his bank for an extension on his overdraft, but his request was denied. With bills piling up, John sought help from an insolvency practitioner.

A False Promise

The insolvency practitioner initially painted a picture of restructuring, claiming that administration could buy John the time needed to sort things out. But after John agreed, the IP swiftly pivoted to liquidation, citing that the company's situation was "too precarious." The IP's fes for initiating and managing the liquidation consumed most of the company's remaining funds.

Impact on the Community

The liquidation meant not just the end of John's business, but also severe impacts on his employees and the wider community. Among his employees was Lisa, a single mum of two who had worked with John for over ten years. She lost her job with only two weeks' notice and no severance. Finding new work in construction, which was slowing down across the region, proved nearly impossible. Lisa ended up relying on food parcels for the first time in her life.

John's company had also been working on local council housing projects—renovating homes for low-income families. When the liquidation went through, these projects were abandoned mid-way. Families who had been told they would move into their refurbished homes were left waiting indefinitely. The ripple effect of the liquidation extended beyond John's workforce; it hit the community hard, leaving behind unfinished homes and broken promises.

John himself was shattered by the experience. He had built his company over 25 years and was well respected in the community. The shame and stress of insolvency took a serious toll on his health, and he struggled with depression. He had hoped the IP would provide a genuine solution to his financial woes, but instead, they had stripped him of everything. The IP moved on to their next case, while John was left picking up the pieces of a life that had revolved around his now-vanished business.

The systemic failures in John's story reflect a broader problem—one where IPs, driven by profit, disregard the human cost of their actions. They present themselves as a lifeline but turn out to be nothing more than an anchor dragging businesses and communities down. It's a betrayal of trust that leaves behind wreckage—companies lost, livelihoods destroyed, and communities fractured. The construction sites that John once managed now stand as empty reminders of what happens when the system fails those it was meant to support.

The Beast that Begbies Built: Systematic Manipulation

Begbies Traynor has firmly established itself as a powerhouse in the UK insolvency industry, with an empire of over 100 offices, sky-high revenue targets, and a business model that ruthlessly prioritises liquidation over recovery. Through an aggressive, unrelenting acquisition strategy, Begbies Traynor has swallowed up countless smaller, once-independent firms, rebranding them as part of the Begbies conglomerate while creating a carefully curated illusion of independence. The result? A lack of competition, fewer genuine options for struggling directors, and an industry that places cold, hard revenue above the livelihoods and futures of business owners and employees.

In this chapter, we dissect how Begbies Traynor's partner pay structures, office expansion tactics, and deceptive branding strategies combine to form an insolvent juggernaut that not only dominates the industry but enforces practices that are actively undermining the UK's economic resilience.

A System Focused on Revenue – How Partner Pay Drives Begbies' Approach

At the heart of Begbies Traynor's system lies its partner pay structure—a model crafted to reward one thing: revenue. The more fees the partners generate, the bigger their payday. The direct link between partner earnings and case revenue means that insolvency practitioners (IPs) are incentivised not to rescue struggling businesses, but to liquidate them and drag out investigations for as long as possible. After all, liquidations and forensic investigations are where the big money is—why help a company recover when gutting it makes you richer?

Profit-Driven Compensation in the Begbies Model

Partners at Begbies Traynor enjoy lucrative revenue-linked bonuses and profit-sharing schemes. Their earnings rise in line with the fees they can squeeze out of every case, creating a culture that sees liquidation not as a last resort but as the easiest, most profitable option. This isn't about saving businesses or helping directors rebuild—this is about maximising fees, pure and simple.

Think about it: an IP could work to create a voluntary arrangement, a compromise that allows the business to continue operating, saving jobs and preserving value. Or they could liquidate—rake in fees for administration, management, asset sales, and a detailed investigation into the company's history. It's not hard to see why liquidation is the favourite child in the Begbies household.

For directors, this means that seeking help from Begbies comes with a pre-packaged risk. The moment they enter the Begbies system, the focus isn't on providing real solutions; it's on how to generate as much revenue from the case as possible. This means pushing liquidation, even when recovery options could potentially save the business.

Expansion by Acquisition – The Illusion of Choice

Begbies Traynor has expanded aggressively across the UK by gobbling up smaller, regional insolvency firms. They don't just rebrand these acquisitions; instead, they keep the original names intact. On the surface, it looks like directors have multiple options—a choice between big players and local independents. But in reality, many of these supposedly "local" firms are simply extensions of the Begbies behemoth.

This acquisition strategy has led to a market saturated by Begbies-controlled entities, all following the same liquidation-focused playbook. The illusion of choice is a brilliant move—a smoke-and-mirrors act that keeps directors believing they've chosen a smaller, friendlier firm when, in reality, they've walked straight into Begbies' grasp.

Creating a False Sense of Independence

When directors reach out to what they think is an independent firm, they are often unaware that it is now part of Begbies' vast machinery. The old, trusted brand names are retained—those logos, those familiar office signs, all stay put. But behind the name lies the same cutthroat Begbies system. This misleading branding strategy exploits the trust directors have in their local firms, pulling them into a corporate structure that cares only for one thing: fees.

Begbies has made a calculated decision here: keep the brand intact to preserve the reputation these smaller firms have built over decades, all the while ensuring that every decision, every process, every partner target aligns with Begbies Traynor's revenue goals. For directors, this removes any real chance of finding support that's actually tailored to recovery—they're being reeled in by a false promise.

An Example of 'In-House Independence'

Imagine you're a director seeking help. You deliberately avoid the big players, opting for what appears to be a smaller, community-focused firm—perhaps one that has been around for decades, a firm your accountant once recommended. What you don't know is that this "independent" office is now under the complete control of Begbies. The staff are trained in Begbies' methods, the partners are bound by Begbies' revenue-driven incentives, and all the operational decisions filter down from Begbies' centralised command. The firm may still have its old name on the door, but everything else is dictated by the Begbies blueprint.

The Deceptive Branding Strategy: A Wolf in Sheep's Clothing

The decision to maintain the branding of acquired firms is not accidental—it's a deliberate strategy that allows Begbies Traynor to create a sprawling network of "independent" providers, which, in truth, are anything but. This deceptive approach is one of the most cynical moves Begbies has made—it capitalises on the reputation of these smaller firms, turning their legacy and their community goodwill into a mere funnel for Begbies' profit-making machine.

Impact on Directors' Decision-Making

For directors in distress, this is more than just misleading—it's a betrayal. They think they're engaging with a small, trusted firm that will genuinely look at all options. Instead, they're drawn into Begbies Traynor's profit-first model without realising it. Their choices aren't choices at all—they're preordained outcomes, meticulously orchestrated by a system built to liquidate first and ask questions never.

Begbies' strategy removes competition from the market while presenting the facade of choice, creating a marketplace where every road, every option, ultimately leads back to them. Directors are faced with what appears to be a diverse set of choices, but in reality, they're stepping into the same machinery that views liquidation as the only viable option.

Begbies' Real Estate Empire – Funding Expansion Through Insolvency Fees

The office portfolio Begbies Traynor has amassed is nothing short of impressive—prime locations from London to Manchester and beyond. It's a symbol of their reach, but more importantly, it's a testament to their need for an ongoing influx of fees. The revenue from liquidation cases funds these offices, creating a feedback loop that demands more and more insolvencies to sustain Begbies' ever-growing empire.

How Real Estate Investment Drives Begbies' Profit Goals

Let's be clear: those offices in central London, those prestigious addresses—they don't come cheap. To maintain these expensive spaces, Begbies needs one thing: a steady stream of insolvency cases generating high fees. Each new office opening, each acquisition, isn't just about expanding reach—it's about expanding their need for more cases, more fees, more liquidations.

Real estate is part of Begbies' branding strategy. It shows power, dominance, and omnipresence in the industry. But those shiny offices are paid for by the fees they extract from struggling businesses—the inflated, unnecessary fees that come with a liquidation-first approach. Directors aren't just paying for insolvency services—they're funding Begbies' real estate pet projects.

A Liquidation-First Mentality – The Begbies Blueprint for Insolvency

At Begbies, liquidation isn't a last resort—it's a first instinct. When IPs are rewarded for the revenue they bring in and when offices require high-fee cases just to keep the lights on, liquidation becomes not just the easiest option, but the most lucrative. The alternatives—like voluntary settlements or restructuring—are more complicated, bring in fewer fees, and don't fit the revenue-driven model. So, liquidation it is, time and time again.

Illustrating the Liquidation Bias Through Case Histories

Look through Begbies Traynor's case histories, and a clear pattern emerges: liquidation, liquidation, liquidation. Cases where restructuring could have worked, where jobs could have been saved, where the business could have continued—thrown by the wayside in favour of the high fees of a quick liquidation. For Begbies, the choice is simple: why support recovery when liquidation is a goldmine?

For directors, it means fewer options and more pressure. They walk into Begbies' offices hoping for support, for guidance on how to rebuild, only to be told that liquidation is the "best way forward"—because for Begbies, it is.

The Market Impact of Begbies' Consolidation

Begbies Traynor's relentless acquisition strategy doesn't just affect the individual directors who fall into their clutches; it reshapes the entire insolvency industry. With fewer truly independent firms left standing, Begbies' liquidation-first approach is becoming the standard across the sector. Small firms that once fought for recovery are now subsidiaries, their focus shifted to match Begbies' profit-driven model.

Consolidation as an Obstacle to Reform

This consolidation isn't just about controlling the market; it's about controlling the narrative. Smaller firms that might have advocated for reform, for recovery-first policies, are now part of the Begbies machine. There is no dissenting voice, no push for change—just a homogenised system that views liquidation as the answer to every question. The lack of diversity stifles innovation, and it means that for directors in distress, genuine recovery options are becoming harder and harder to find.

Exposing the Begbies Blueprint

Begbies Traynor's business model is a stark example of everything that's wrong with the UK's insolvency industry. Partner-driven revenue targets, real estate-funded expansion, deceptive acquisitions—each element works in tandem to create a system that enriches Begbies at the expense of those it's supposed to serve.

As the UK insolvency landscape becomes increasingly dominated by Begbies Traynor and its network of pseudo-independent subsidiaries, the need for reform grows more urgent by the day. This consolidation has shifted the balance of power, allowing Begbies to set the agenda, normalise exorbitant fees, and shape the future of insolvency practice in ways that harm rather than help.

The truth is simple: the more power Begbies consolidates, the less room there is for genuine recovery. The system has been twisted into a profit-driven monster, and unless it is challenged, unless transparency and fairness are restored, Begbies will continue to feed off the remains of struggling businesses—leaving nothing but a trail of closures, lost jobs, and shattered futures in its wake.

A System of Retribution, Not Re-education

In the UK, directors of insolvent companies don't just face the financial collapse of their businesses—they are thrown headfirst into a legal system that seems designed to punish them for daring to try. Rather than focusing on re-education or constructive oversight, the insolvency process subjects directors to exhaustive investigations, relentless questioning, and potential legal penalties for even the most mundane infractions. This culture of retribution creates a climate of fear and discouragement for entrepreneurs, sending an unmistakable message: mess up, even slightly, and we'll make your life a living hell, whether you deserve it or not.

This chapter will explore how the UK's insolvency system enforces this punitive approach, how lengthy investigations serve as a cash cow for insolvency practitioners (IPs), and why, even when no misconduct is proven, directors are still forced to endure this gruelling ordeal.

The Punitive Framework of UK Insolvency Law

UK insolvency laws are supposedly there to protect creditors and maintain order. But in reality, they've built a playground where every director of an insolvent company becomes prey, ripe for picking. The Insolvency Act of 1986, along with subsequent regulations, was ostensibly designed to prevent fraudulent or reckless actions that harm creditors. But let's face it, these laws are wielded like blunt instruments, turning every director into a suspect and subjecting them to a financial inquisition that seems more about justifying fees than ensuring justice.

The very moment a company enters liquidation, directors are put under a microscope—only it's more like a magnifying glass, and they're the ants. IPs, armed with broad discretion, dig through years of financial records, scrutinising every decision, every payment, every invoice—looking for that single mistake they can wave triumphantly as if they've just uncovered a criminal conspiracy. Most of the time, they're not looking for fraud—they're looking for an excuse to bill more hours. And they do so without mercy. Even if they find nothing, the process itself is the punishment. The longer it lasts, the more the IP profits, like a mechanic "fixing" a car that was never really broken to begin with.

Statistics on Investigations and Disqualification Rates

The numbers reveal a bleak, almost dystopian reality about the insolvency investigation process in the UK:

- **Over 75% of insolvent company directors** face formal investigations by IPs. And yet, a tiny percentage of these directors are actually disqualified. During the 2022/23 financial year, the Insolvency Service obtained just **932 director disqualifications**—a small slice of those facing investigation. So, the real outcome? The majority of directors endure gruelling, exhaustive inquiries only to be cleared. But by the end, many have already been emotionally and financially gutted. The process is like being accused of a crime, forced through trial, and found innocent—but you're still slapped with the legal bill and psychological scars.

- **The average cost of an IP-led investigation** keeps rising, with directors left footing the bill, both in terms of finances and the personal cost of being subjected to an unrelenting, Kafkaesque interrogation. The investigation phase, rather than any actual misconduct, is where IPs make their money. They bill for every interview, every piece of paperwork, every hour spent pondering whether your choice to buy office plants in 2017 was fiscally irresponsible.

The Process as Punishment

For many directors, the real ordeal isn't the final judgment; it's the relentless scrutiny. Every decision made in the years leading up to insolvency is subject to an inquisition—an endless series of questions that make even the most mundane business decision seem like an act of high treason. Imagine every choice you've ever made in business, every supplier you've ever paid, every bill you deferred to make payroll—all of it pulled apart by someone whose only incentive is to keep the meter running.

Consider David, a director of a small tech company that collapsed after a major client unexpectedly withdrew. He did everything he could—delayed his own salary, cut costs—but it wasn't enough. When the company went into liquidation, the IP flagged David's deferred salary as potentially "preferential." For months, David faced repeated interviews, document requests, and accusations over financial decisions that could have been taken from "Managing a Company for Dummies." The IP found no misconduct. But David came out the other side broken—financially and mentally. His punishment wasn't a conviction or disqualification; it was the drawn-out torment of the investigation itself. Meanwhile, the IP comfortably padded their wallet by billing for each pointless hour spent examining whether David bought too much printer ink in 2019.

The Role of IPs in Prolonging Investigations

For insolvency practitioners, every extra day an investigation drags on means more billable hours, more fees, more money. Why conclude an investigation in two months when you could draw it out for twelve? Every hour spent examining records, every prolonged interview, every piece of correspondence—it all translates to profit. The system hands IPs a perfect incentive to turn every straightforward investigation into an archaeological dig through the ruins of someone's failed dreams.

This isn't about finding the truth. It's about keeping the hamster wheel spinning just fast enough to justify those hourly fees. Directors, meanwhile, are left in a nightmare—a bureaucratic purgatory with no idea if or when they'll ever be set free.

Statistics on IP Fees and Investigation Costs

The financial damage speaks for itself. Insolvency practitioners typically charge **five or six figures on average per CVL** for investigation and asset realisation alone. According to the Insolvency Service, investigations account for up to **40% of total IP fees** in some cases. To directors, these fees aren't just numbers—they're the shards of a shattered life, the money that could have been spent on rebuilding, on therapy, on moving on. Instead, they were forked over to IPs who found yet another reason to check if that expense from three years ago was legit.

The Emotional and Financial Toll on Directors

The investigation process is an all-out assault—financially, emotionally, and psychologically. Directors are already devastated by the collapse of their businesses, and the investigation only deepens the wound. Each interaction with the IP feels like a new accusation, a relentless reminder of their perceived incompetence. Imagine what that does to a person. Imagine every email, every letter, every probing question making you feel like a criminal when all you tried to do was keep the lights on.

Take Amber, a director of a boutique retail business that entered liquidation. She faced a prolonged investigation in which every payment she made in the last two years was scrutinised. Rent payments, supplier invoices—each one was flagged, turned into yet another chargeable hour for the IP. Each query was just another excuse to tack on more fees. Despite Amber's full cooperation, the investigation dragged on for nearly a year. Though she was eventually cleared, she emerged with nothing—no business, no savings, just an inbox full of emails from the IP and a haunting sense that her life had been hijacked.

The Broader Impact: Discouraging Entrepreneurship and Innovation

This punitive, profit-driven approach doesn't just destroy individual lives—it sends a chilling message across the business landscape. Directors who endure this ordeal often vow never to take another risk. The knowledge that even the best-intentioned mistake could lead to months of invasive scrutiny is enough to make any would-be entrepreneur think twice. It tells them: "Don't you dare dream too big. Because if you fail, we will ruin you, even if you played by the rules."

In countries where insolvency isn't used as a blunt instrument to crush the human spirit, entrepreneurs are free to fail and try again. Failure is seen as part of growth—a stepping stone. But in the UK, the only growth is the IP's bank balance. The system's obsession with punishment suppresses the very innovation and risk-taking that drives progress, that creates jobs, that fuels the economy.

Comparative Insight

Consider this: a study comparing insolvency outcomes across Europe found that in countries like Germany and the Netherlands, which have more recovery-focused systems, over 60% of insolvent businesses were able to restructure and continue operations. In the UK, that figure is less than 15%. We're not just failing directors—we're failing as an economy, as a society. We're prioritising liquidation and punishment over resilience and growth. The UK's system is so focused on penalising directors that it fails to see the value in nurturing those who, given the chance, could rebuild.

More on this later...

A System in Need of Reform: From Retribution to Constructive Oversight

The current insolvency system isn't just failing directors—it's failing creditors, employees, and the entire economy. Accountability is one thing, but the emphasis on punitive, protracted investigations serves nobody but the IPs. Directors who are cleared of wrongdoing still emerge from the process financially crippled and emotionally hollowed out. They pay the price for a system designed to punish rather than reform.

A reformed insolvency system would strike a balance between accountability and support. Instead of focusing on finding tiny mistakes to justify dragging out investigations, the process should aim to help directors learn, adapt, and try again. Constructive oversight, rather than punitive punishment, would protect creditors, support directors, and ultimately benefit the economy as a whole. A director allowed to recover, who is given the tools to learn from failure, will contribute more to society than one crushed under the weight of a bloated investigation process.

Conclusion: The Process as Punishment

In the UK's insolvency framework, **the process itself is the punishment**. Directors are subjected to endless scrutiny, forced to justify decisions made in times of crisis, and saddled with exorbitant fees. For IPs, prolonging these investigations is a lucrative business. For directors, it's a never-ending nightmare—a punishment that leaves them broken, even if they did nothing wrong.

This emphasis on punishment over reeducation is suppressing innovation, discouraging risk-taking, and ultimately stifling economic growth. As we continue to dissect the machinery of the UK's insolvency industry, it's clear that reform isn't just desirable—it's necessary. A system focused on constructive oversight, rather than needless punishment, would support directors, stimulate entrepreneurship, and foster a more resilient economy. In the next chapter, we'll explore the pervasive fear that keeps directors from speaking out, and why IPs are allowed to operate with impunity.

The Fear Factor: Why Directors Won't Speak Out

In a fair system, those who feel wronged should be able to speak up, share their experiences, and seek justice. In the UK's insolvency industry, however, there is a pervasive culture of silence. Directors rarely voice their grievances against the process, even when they feel mistreated, overcharged, or unjustly scrutinised. The reasons for this silence are complex but boil down to a potent blend of social stigma, the overwhelming power of the insolvency practitioners (IPs), and the industry's tight grip on power.

In this chapter, we'll uncover why directors—even when they're screaming inside—choose to keep their heads down. Because when the options are getting screwed quietly or drawing attention to yourself while getting screwed, most people choose the former. This culture of silence perpetuates a power imbalance that suits the industry perfectly but fails society in every possible way.

Avoiding Public Scrutiny: Fear of Social Stigma

For many directors, the social fallout of insolvency is worse than the financial one. In the UK, bankruptcy and liquidation aren't just seen as business mishaps—they're social stains, the kind you can't wash off. Failure is a public affair here, and the shame of being "the guy who tanked his own company" sticks around long after the creditors have moved on. Directors know this. They know that their name will be forever linked with failure. The neighbours will whisper, their friends will throw them sympathetic looks, and the aunt who always thought they were too ambitious to open a

Polynesian Tapas Bar just off the A10 will suddenly be proven right. And no one wants to give that cow the satisfaction.

Highlighting their experiences in a public dispute only draws more attention to what they'd prefer to bury. The insolvency already put a spotlight on their failure, but raising complaints would be like turning on floodlights. Family, friends, former employees—everyone gets a front-row seat to watch you argue about just how badly you were mistreated after you already went under. Many directors would rather swallow the injustice than invite everyone to examine it with a magnifying glass.

In a society that still equates business failure with personal incompetence, directors often choose to endure mistreatment in silence rather than draw even more attention to themselves. And why wouldn't they? In a world where success is the only acceptable currency, anything that smells like failure is enough to get you thrown out of the club.

An Uneven Playing Field: IPs' Vast Resources Make Resistance Seem Pointless

Speaking of getting thrown out of the club, let's talk about the absolute lack of fairness when it comes to challenging an IP. On one side, you have directors—financially wrecked, emotionally spent, and just trying to navigate what's left of their lives. On the other, you've got IPs—aided by vast legal teams, sophisticated accounting tools, and coffers stuffed with the spoils of past insolvencies. It's like a boxer with two broken hands trying to take on a heavyweight champion armed with brass knuckles.

IPs operate in well-funded firms that eat legal challenges for breakfast. When directors consider challenging an IP's actions, they're up against an organisation with deep pockets, connections, and the resources to drag things out until the director is left with nothing but a bitter aftertaste and an even emptier bank account. Every hour of legal work that the IP's legal team bills for is just another charge on the insolvent estate—meaning the director's own business is paying for its demise. And if they're feeling particularly vindictive, they'll even try to bill the director personally. It's a lose-lose situation for directors—one that they can't afford to take on.

So directors just keep their heads down, hoping not to get noticed. They know that even if they're right, the fight could cost them what little they have left. And if they lose, they could end up even deeper in the hole, staring at a fresh pile of legal bills with nowhere left to turn. The prospect of fighting an unwinnable battle against an opponent with every advantage isn't just daunting—it's absurd. Better to walk away than risk another round with a professional profit-extractor who has nothing but time and resources on their side.

Powerful Connections: The Influence of IPs in the Corridors of Power

It's not just about the resources. The power of IPs goes beyond big bank accounts and well-paid lawyers. Many of the larger IP firms maintain cosy relationships with government bodies, regulators, and the sort of people who decide how the rules work. These connections are what makes the insolvency world turn, ensuring that IPs remain untouchable, even when their actions are shady at best and predatory at worst.

Directors know that these aren't just business relationships—they're part of an interconnected web of influence that shields IPs from scrutiny. Imagine it: you're a director who wants to complain that an IP overcharged or mishandled your case. You start to dig, and suddenly you realise the person you're complaining about knows your regulator, your lawyer, even the guy who gives out the business licenses. It doesn't take long before you realise just how badly the cards are stacked against you. It's not just that the game is rigged—it's that the gamekeeper is best mates with the other team.

The last thing a director wants is to bring down the wrath of that network on their heads. Speaking out could lead to all sorts of unpleasant repercussions—regulators taking a sudden interest in their affairs, industry bodies deciding to "review" their activities, and former connections closing off opportunities. It's a lose-lose situation, and every director knows it. Better to swallow the injustice, keep your head down, and try to stay out of the spotlight than take on an opponent who has the power to ruin your career for a second time.

A System Designed to Silence

When you add up the fear of social stigma, the intimidating resources of IPs, and the industry's powerful connections, you get a system designed to keep directors muzzled. Directors already feel defeated by the collapse of their business, but the prospect of taking on an IP—one armed with seemingly infinite resources and untouchable connections—is too much. It's David versus Goliath if Goliath had an army of lawyers, a couple of politicians in his pocket, and an unlimited expense account.

The result? IPs operate with near impunity. They can overcharge, they can prolong investigations, they can maximise their own profit at the expense of creditors and directors—and they know they'll rarely face consequences. Why? Because the people who could complain are too afraid to do so. The deck is stacked, the house always wins, and the directors have no choice but to walk away.

Statistics on IP Complaints and Director Silence

The numbers don't lie. According to the Insolvency Service, fewer than 1% of insolvency cases result in formal complaints against IPs. Compare that to a University of Nottingham study which found that over 30% of directors expressed dissatisfaction with how their cases were handled. That's a pretty stark disconnect between how many directors feel mistreated and how many actually make their voices heard. The system isn't designed to handle complaints; it's designed to make sure they never see the light of day.

Case Studies in Silence

Take James, a director of a concept restaurant that went under after a key investor pulled out. During liquidation, James felt like he was being bled dry by IP fees, and that the firm wasn't even trying to rescue the business—just flogging it for parts. He thought about making some noise, maybe raising a complaint. But then he realised: what would that do? Friends and family would only see headlines about his failed company, and no one would care about the finer details of the insolvency abuse. Did James want to broadcast his failure on a louder speaker just to argue about the size of the screw that was used to nail his coffin shut? He kept his head down, bit his tongue, and tried to rebuild his life without anyone knowing just how hard he'd been shafted.

Then there's Clare, who ran a makeup company that collapsed thanks to rising costs and bad timing. She wanted to challenge the IP's tactics—she felt they'd needlessly stretched out the investigation to rack up more fees. But when Clare thought about what that would actually mean—going head-to-head with a firm that had an army of accountants and lawyers—she realised it was futile. She'd run out of fight, out of money, and out of options. So, Clare did what the system expects of her—she backed down, paid up, and tried to move on with what little dignity she had left.

These aren't rare cases—they're the norm. Directors are silenced not by direct threats, but by the unspoken certainty that the consequences of fighting back are just too high. The risks aren't worth it, and the chance of success is next to nil.

The Impact of Silence: How It Shields the Industry from Reform

This culture of silence does more than just protect IPs from being held accountable—it prevents any real change. Directors are too scared to speak, so policymakers are left in the dark. They don't hear about the overcharging, the exploitation, the extortionate fees, and the emotional toll—so they don't act. The IP industry, meanwhile, gets to sit back, secure in the knowledge that the people it's supposed to serve will never challenge its authority. It's the perfect system: insulated from criticism, protected by a wall of fear, and accountable to no one but itself.

The insolvency industry maintains a monopoly on the narrative, and any director who might provide a different story is silenced before they can even start. As long as directors stay scared, the industry can continue operating as it always has—profiting from misery, unchecked, and unchallenged.

Breaking the Silence: Empowering Directors to Speak Out

The only way to change this rigged game is to give directors a way to speak out without fear of losing even more. Here's how that could start:

1. **Confidential Reporting Mechanisms**: An anonymous platform for directors to report IP abuses, overseen by an independent authority, could let directors voice concerns without risking retaliation.

2. **Protections Against Retaliation**: Legal shields to ensure directors who speak out aren't targeted by IPs, regulators, or anyone else looking to make their lives even more miserable.

3. **Awareness Campaigns**: Let's teach directors about their rights during insolvency—knowledge is power, and right now, directors are fighting blind.

4. **Transparent Oversight**: A truly independent regulatory body, untainted by industry ties, dedicated to holding IPs accountable.

5. **Media Engagement**: Work with the media to dismantle the stigma of insolvency—highlight directors who've successfully challenged abuse to make speaking out less terrifying.

Exposing the Culture of Silence

The insolvency industry's biggest asset isn't its army of lawyers or its influence in high places—it's the silence of the directors it preys upon. The culture of silence keeps directors scared, keeps the truth buried, and keeps IPs free from consequence. If directors could share their experiences without fear, we'd see the ugly truth behind the insolvency industry laid bare, and maybe—just maybe—reform would finally follow.

By addressing this culture of silence, the UK could take its first steps toward an insolvency system that genuinely values fairness, accountability, and transparency. Only by empowering directors to speak out can we hope to create an insolvency landscape that serves the public interest instead of the private profit of a few well-connected vultures.

In the next chapter, we'll discuss how we're to deal with crooks. There are some bad apples out there who need jailing, but if a friendly IP ain't going to do it – then who should?

What to Do with the Crooks? A New Approach to Investigations in Insolvency

Insolvency practitioners (IPs) love to tell you they're the heroes keeping the UK economy safe from all those shadowy fraudsters and rogue directors. Without them, they say, the UK would be nothing more than a playground for crooks and conmen. They talk a good game, highlighting the few times they've caught a director with their hands in the till, using these rare cases to paint themselves as the protectors of business ethics.

But let's be real. The vast majority of directors who go through insolvency haven't done anything illegal. They're not trying to scam anyone—they're just people who took a shot, made some bad bets, or got caught off-guard by a market that decided to pull the rug out from under them. Even when there is evidence of misconduct, the idea of giving IPs free reign to investigate, while they also stand to profit handsomely from doing so, is like letting the fox guard the henhouse. The real solution isn't to give these powers to profit-driven private actors; it's to create a system that's actually fair—one that aims to protect the public without milking struggling directors dry.

A System Rooted in Profit, Not Justice

IPs are given some pretty extraordinary powers under UK law. When a company collapses, they can dive into years of financial records, rummaging around like overenthusiastic detectives, questioning everything from petty cash payments to the time you bought biscuits for the office. Their job, ostensibly, is to find evidence of fraud or any action that didn't serve the best interests of creditors. Sounds noble, right?

Well, sure—except they're not doing this out of the goodness of their hearts. Unlike a government body that might investigate for the public good, IPs do it for profit. Every email, every letter, every hour spent hunting for wrongdoing gets billed back to the insolvent estate. It doesn't matter if they're chasing an actual crook or just a well-meaning director who made a bad decision—it's all about how many hours they can log.

So, what we end up with is a system where IPs have every reason to treat every director as if they're guilty until proven otherwise. They get to squeeze every last drop of profit out of a company that's already on its knees. And when they finally hand down their verdict, even if it's, "Oops, looks like there was no misconduct here," the fees still get paid, and it's the director who's left to foot the bill.

I've seen it firsthand—directors dragged through the mud for completely legitimate decisions, all because the IP was motivated to find something, anything, they could question. These people aren't criminals. They're entrepreneurs who took a chance, and sometimes that chance didn't pay off. Treating them like crooks just because it's profitable isn't justice; it's exploitation on an industrial scale.

Government-Led Investigations: Why Public Agencies Should Take Over

If the goal is genuinely to catch fraud, why are we leaving it to private, profit-driven firms? Public agencies like HM Revenue and Customs (HMRC) or the police are far better suited to the task. These are organisations that already have the tools to detect dodgy business practices. HMRC, for example, can already spot financial irregularities and unpaid taxes—why not let them take the lead when a company goes under?

Unlike IPs, government bodies aren't interested in turning a profit. They've got a job to do: protect the public, enforce the law, and ensure fairness. If they took over the role of investigating insolvency cases, we could actually have a system that treats directors fairly. They would be able to make the distinction between actual criminal behaviour and simple mistakes. Not every delayed payment is a fraud scheme; sometimes it's just a director trying to juggle a bit of cash flow.

Imagine HMRC taking a good, hard look at a company's books. If they spot something criminal, they can bring in the police—actual law enforcement, not some guy billing you £400 an hour to find out why you spent £3.50 on a stapler. And if the police find evidence of fraud? Great—lock the fraudster up and throw away the key. But if it's just a director who made a couple of bad calls, maybe give them a nudge in the right direction rather than a boot in the teeth.

The Benefits of a Public Investigation Model: Less Bias, Less Exploitation

Handing over the investigation responsibilities to public bodies wouldn't just be fairer—it would be smarter. Here's why:

1. **No Profit Motive**: HMRC and the police don't need to inflate their workloads just to meet revenue targets. They're there to uphold the law, not rake in cash.

Investigations would be driven by the merits of the case, not by how much can be squeezed out of it.

2. **Accountability**: Public agencies are overseen by, well, the public. They're accountable. When they screw up, there's a system to call them out on it. Compare that to IPs, who operate with minimal oversight and have personal incentives woven into every decision they make.

3. **Freeing Up IPs to Actually Do Their Job**: If IPs weren't so busy pretending to be the FBI, they could focus on their actual job—winding down the company, paying out creditors, and doing it efficiently. By taking the investigative role out of their hands, we'd see faster, fairer insolvency proceedings.

4. **Financial Relief for Directors**: Under the current system, directors can end up on the hook for massive investigation fees, even if they've done nothing wrong. Handing investigations over to public bodies means directors won't be financially ruined just because an IP needed to hit their billing quota.

Re-education, Not Retribution: A New Way to Approach Business Mistakes

Let's face it: business is a risky game. You win some, you lose some, and sometimes you lose so badly that the game ends right there, on the spot. But does that mean every mistake deserves punishment? Should every misstep result in financial ruin or, worse, legal consequences? Of course not. Most directors aren't malevolent masterminds plotting corporate heists. They're just regular people who made a judgment call that didn't pay off. Instead of punishing them, why not give them the tools to do better next time?

That's where re-education comes in. Instead of a punitive system that strips these directors of their dignity and their livelihoods, we could build a framework that helps them learn from their mistakes, equips them with the knowledge they need, and sends them back into the economy stronger and wiser. Below, we'll explore some of the types of re-education that should be offered for directors who find themselves on the wrong side of civil law—not because they were deceitful, but because they were unprepared, inexperienced, or simply unlucky.

Financial Literacy Programs: Teaching Directors to Navigate Cash Flow and Capital

The most common reason businesses fail isn't fraud, malfeasance, or embezzlement—it's simple cash flow mismanagement. Cash flow is the lifeblood of any company, and when it's not handled properly, even the most promising enterprises can go under. Yet many directors are not accountants. They start their businesses with a great idea, a passion, a vision—but without necessarily knowing how to manage the books.

A re-education initiative focused on financial literacy could be a game-changer. Directors who ran into trouble because they misunderstood cash flow dynamics should be enrolled in intensive workshops where they learn how to manage working capital, balance incoming and outgoing payments, and anticipate potential shortfalls before they become disastrous. It could be as simple as understanding the importance of a cash reserve or knowing when to negotiate payment terms with suppliers.

Imagine how different things could be if, instead of treating cash flow issues as a crime, we treated them as a solvable problem. Directors could emerge with a far better grasp of financial planning, knowing when and how to pivot before things reach a breaking point. For many, this kind of training could mean the difference between falling back into insolvency and turning their next venture into a success story.

Regulatory Compliance Training: Helping Directors Stay on the Right Side of the Rules

Regulatory compliance is another area where many directors get tripped up. The UK's business regulations are a labyrinth, a twisting maze of rules, standards, and requirements that even experienced directors struggle to navigate. And let's be honest—most directors don't set out to break the rules; they just don't always understand them, or they underestimate their complexity.

A structured regulatory compliance training program could help directors understand their obligations more clearly. This wouldn't be about turning them into legal experts—no one expects a director to suddenly become fluent in the language of government regulation. Instead, these programs could offer practical training on the key regulatory challenges that directors commonly face, such as filing deadlines, tax obligations, and industry-specific standards.

The goal is to prevent the type of minor non-compliance that often gets highlighted by IPs during investigations. If a director accidentally missed a statutory deadline, they shouldn't have to endure a year of being hunted like they're the next Bernie Madoff. They should be educated about the importance of regulatory timeliness, and equipped with tools—like planning software and checklists—that make compliance easier and more intuitive.

Corporate Governance and Ethical Decision-Making: Building Stronger Leadership Skills

Corporate governance and ethical decision-making are areas that can also be addressed through re-education. Many directors, particularly those who started out as entrepreneurs, have never been formally trained in how to run a board, how to manage conflicts of interest, or how to navigate difficult ethical choices in business. As a result, they might make governance mistakes—not out of malice, but simply out of ignorance or inexperience.

Rather than punishing these directors, we could offer them targeted training programs on effective corporate governance. These sessions could teach the core principles of running a board, the importance of maintaining separation between personal and business finances, and how to ensure that every decision made is in the best interests of the company and its stakeholders.

Think of this as building a foundation of strong ethical leadership—because that's what's really needed. Directors who receive governance training can go on to lead companies in ways that are fairer, more transparent, and better for everyone involved. They can be equipped with strategies for navigating ethical gray areas, taught how to identify potential conflicts before they escalate, and given a roadmap for ensuring that company actions are always above board.

Crisis Management and Contingency Planning: Preparing Directors for the Unexpected

If there's one thing that's guaranteed in business, it's that things will not go according to plan. Markets fluctuate, key clients pull out, pandemics strike—the list goes on. And yet, many directors enter business without a realistic plan for managing crises. When things go wrong, they panic, make rushed decisions, and sometimes dig their businesses into even deeper holes.

This is where crisis management training could be invaluable. Directors need to be taught not just how to create a contingency plan, but how to remain calm and rational when everything seems to be going wrong. They need to learn how to assess their options, take a step back, and act in a way that's calculated rather than reactionary. Contingency planning sessions could focus on practical skills like setting up emergency cash reserves, negotiating with creditors under pressure, and finding opportunities in the midst of setbacks.

By offering this kind of training, we could reduce the number of directors who make poor decisions simply because they didn't know what else to do. They'd learn to approach crises with a cool head, ensuring that fewer businesses collapse due to rash, panicked decisions when times get tough.

Leadership and Employee Relations: Creating Resilient Teams

Another aspect of running a successful company, which often gets overlooked in the race to hit targets and manage cash flow, is the importance of strong employee relations and leadership. Directors who have never led a team before can sometimes make poor calls regarding staff—whether that's failing to communicate during tough times, mishandling redundancies, or not leveraging the skills of their employees effectively.

Leadership and employee relations training could help directors become better leaders. This might include teaching them effective communication strategies, methods for fostering team morale even during financial stress, and skills for conducting difficult conversations—like announcing pay cuts or negotiating with employees about working hours.

When a company faces challenges, it's often the employees who are the greatest asset in turning things around. Directors who understand how to lead people through difficulty are far better positioned to navigate insolvency and come out the other side intact. The focus should be on showing directors how to build a resilient, motivated workforce that can help them weather the toughest business storms.

Strategic Decision-Making and Long-Term Planning: Looking Beyond the Short-Term Gain

Insolvency often results from a series of short-term decisions made without fully considering their long-term implications. Whether it's taking on debt to finance immediate growth, ignoring mounting tax liabilities to pay a pressing supplier, or failing to diversify revenue streams, these decisions are usually made in good faith but with poor strategic foresight.

Courses in strategic decision-making and long-term planning could help directors gain a better understanding of how their choices today affect their company's future. By learning how to create realistic business plans, set achievable goals, and balance risk and reward, directors would be less likely to steer their companies into dangerous waters. They could be taught how to spot early warning signs of trouble and how to pivot their strategy before things spiral out of control.

This kind of education isn't about eliminating risk—no business can do that—but it is about making sure directors understand the full scope of the risks they are taking on and that they have a clear plan for navigating them. This isn't just good for directors; it's good for creditors, employees, and the entire business community.

Re-education: Building a Stronger Economy

Ultimately, the idea behind re-education is simple: rather than punishing people for mistakes, let's help them learn from those mistakes. Most directors are not bad actors; they're just people who, in a moment of crisis, made a poor choice or didn't have the knowledge they needed to make the right one. By investing in re-education, we could transform a punitive system into a supportive one—one that encourages resilience, innovation, and growth.

Instead of creating a business environment where directors are too afraid of the consequences to take risks, we'd be fostering a culture that says: "Take the risk, and if it doesn't work out, we'll help you learn and do better next time." The cost of offering this kind of education would be far outweighed by the benefits—fewer business failures, more successful entrepreneurs, and an economy that's willing to take the risks necessary for innovation.

A system that punishes minor mistakes with financial ruin isn't just harsh; it's self-defeating. We can't grow an economy that's unwilling to tolerate failure. By replacing punishment with education, we can create a system where directors emerge from adversity not broken, but rebuilt—smarter, stronger, and ready to contribute again. Now that's a system worth striving for.

The Insolvency Practitioners' Defence – A Narrative of Self-Preservation

Insolvency practitioners (IPs) occupy a contentious space within the UK's economic framework. They portray themselves as the stewards of financial order—navigating the complexities of failing companies while supposedly protecting the interests of creditors, employees, and even the directors they interrogate. According to their polished narrative, they bring professionalism and order to the messiness of corporate demise. They claim that Creditors' Voluntary Liquidations (CVLs) are essential for maintaining dignity amidst financial collapse.

What a beautiful story. Unfortunately, like many beautiful stories, it's pure fiction—a bedtime tale that soothes everyone except those who actually live through the nightmare. Behind this perfectly curated image lies an entirely different reality—one I have witnessed countless times in my career advising distressed businesses. The truth? The insolvency industry is a ravenous beast driven by a relentless pursuit of fees. Their incentives are fundamentally misaligned with the public good. What they call a structured, dignified exit for a failing business is, in fact, a calculated and predatory exercise in extracting every last penny, often from the pockets of those who can least afford it. They say they act in the interests of creditors, but the true beneficiaries are themselves, and the economic fallout for the broader community is catastrophic.

The Industry's Defence: The Fairy Tale of the Insolvency Industry

The arguments IPs present, on the surface, seem reasonable enough—like a wolf trying to convince you it's just a misunderstood vegetarian. They position themselves as guardians of financial propriety, insisting that their intervention is necessary for the orderly winding-down of failing companies. They say they are there to prevent chaos, to provide dignity to directors, to protect creditors, and to ensure employees receive what they're due. They argue that without their sacred intervention, the financial resolution of distressed companies would devolve into bedlam, leaving creditors out in the cold with empty pockets and broken promises.

According to their bedtime story, CVLs offer a neat and responsible way to wrap up failing businesses, and IPs claim their expertise ensures an equitable handling of assets. Sounds lovely, doesn't it? Except, like a bad magic trick, when you look behind the curtain, there's nothing there but deception. What they call "structured" is merely a carefully orchestrated looting spree, aimed at maximising their own fees while throwing a few coins to creditors for show.

In practice, IPs have a different priority altogether: themselves. They are incentivised to drag out the process as long as possible, billing the estate for every hour they work. "We protect creditors," they proclaim. Sure, just like Herod "protected" those boys in the Bible. Protecting creditors, in IP lingo, means ensuring their own fees are paid before anyone else gets so much as a crumb. The unsecured creditors? They're lucky to get whatever's left at the bottom of the barrel, and even that might be nicked on the way out. IPs are like pickpockets with a licence—they're not there to protect anyone but themselves.

"Dignity" for Directors: A Euphemism for Financial Evisceration

Let's talk about "dignity"—another favourite word in the IP narrative. Insolvency practitioners like to claim that CVLs offer a dignified exit for directors. This is where their narrative gets especially creative, verging on absurd. CVLs are sold as a responsible, proactive step for directors—a demonstration of facing reality, wrapping up loose ends, and walking away with heads held high. Sounds almost noble, right? Like a Viking funeral for your failing business.

The truth? It's less a dignified exit and more of a prolonged autopsy—with the director lying on the table while the IP dissects every decision they've ever made. "Dignity," in the insolvency world, is really just code for opening up your financial entrails for examination, having someone poke through them while billing you by the hour. The IP isn't there to help; they're there to find any possible excuse to delve into your past transactions, justifying additional investigations and—surprise!—more fees. What they call "dignity" is an extended witch hunt, often lasting years, during which the director's personal finances, and often their sanity, hang in the balance.

The Myth of Economic Stability: Slaughtering Businesses to Save Them

And then we have the pièce de résistance of IP propaganda: the claim that they contribute to economic stability. Apparently, by winding down failing businesses, they're heroes protecting the economy from "zombie companies"— you know, those unprofitable, undead businesses that wander aimlessly through the economic landscape.

According to IPs, they're just cleaning up the mess, freeing up economic resources, and helping the market flourish.

The truth is somewhat darker. In practice, IPs are more like hunters, prowling for wounded prey. They kill off businesses that might have otherwise been saved, simply because liquidation is the fastest way to cash out their fees. They push directors into CVLs because it's easy money—forget restructuring, forget turnaround plans. When you have an industry driven by fee generation, the incentive is always to reach for the low-hanging fruit. Businesses that might have a fighting chance are often pushed into the grinder because the IP needs to pay the bills.

The "economic stability" argument is a sick joke. Instead of stabilising anything, they create an environment of fear. Directors are scared to take risks, terrified of the vultures that will circle if they falter. IPs argue they are protecting the economy, but in reality, they're stifling it, tearing down small businesses to feed their own profit machine while discouraging entrepreneurs from even trying.

The So-Called Regulation of IPs: Foxes Guarding the Henhouse

IPs are fond of pointing to the regulations that supposedly keep them in line. They speak of licensing, oversight, and fee scrutiny as if these elements create an unbreachable fortress of integrity. It's a great talking point for public relations—if only it were true.

The regulatory landscape is, in reality, a comfortable illusion. The oversight bodies that supposedly keep IPs in check are mostly toothless tigers. They're like a night watchman armed with a torch—there's lots of waving it about, but no real consequences. The industry is largely self-regulating, and its vested interests are well protected. On the rare occasion that someone is caught bending the rules, the penalties are about as harsh as a slap on the wrist with a wet noodle. If this is regulation, it's regulation designed to keep IPs in profit, not to protect directors, creditors, or employees.

Employees: "Protections" That Feel More Like Exploitation

Let's not forget the IP's most disingenuous argument of all—their supposed concern for employees. They like to say that by following the formal CVL process, they ensure employees are treated fairly, that redundancy payments are properly handled, and that government support kicks in smoothly. It sounds very compassionate. Except it's not. It's corporate virtue-signalling, and anyone who's been on the receiving end of it knows it's a charade.

Employees lose their jobs—abruptly and without any real consideration for the future. Sure, there's a formal process, but it's akin to someone gently laying flowers at a graveside they dug. The IP moves through the steps, ticks the boxes, and moves on—leaving the employees to fend for themselves in the fallout. The promise of a "formal redundancy process" means little when your job is gone, and you're left wondering how to pay rent while the IP invoices for another ten grand. The only real beneficiary in this process is the IP, who walks away with a fat cheque while employees and their families deal with the wreckage.

A System Rigged for Short-Term Gain, Not Long-Term Stability

Look closely, and you see a system that's all about short-term profit—no depth, no nuance, just a straight-up cash grab. Everything the insolvency industry says about creating economic stability, ensuring dignified exits, and supporting employees boils down to maximising their own fees. Every move they make is calculated for immediate gain, with no thought for the long-term consequences for businesses, directors, employees, or the broader economy.

The UK's economic system needs entrepreneurs who are willing to take risks, to innovate, to dare to build something new. But why would anyone take that risk when the punishment for failure is so severe? The current insolvency system turns failure into a death sentence, not just for businesses, but for the spirit of entrepreneurship itself. We need to embrace the reality of business: risk. Not every venture will succeed, but we should be making it easier for those who fail to dust themselves off and try again—not handing them over to IPs for a financial crucifixion.

The Human Cost of the IP Profit Machine

The saddest part is that all of this is entirely avoidable. I've seen businesses saved—when they've been given the chance. I've helped directors negotiate directly with creditors, restructure their debts, and come out stronger on the other side. But those successes happen not because of the insolvency industry, but in spite of it. When an IP gets involved, the outcome is depressingly predictable: liquidation, asset sales, and the inevitable fee extraction process. It's about hitting the lowest common denominator, cashing out the easiest assets, and ensuring the IP's payday.

Imagine a construction company—skilled employees, valuable contracts, and a director ready to fight for survival. Instead of receiving support, they find themselves at the mercy of an IP who quickly shuts the whole thing down. Why? Because liquidation is faster, easier, and more profitable for the IP. And so, the contracts vanish, the jobs disappear, and the local community is left with nothing but the ruins of a business that could have been saved. The director is left to fend off personal claims while the IP cashes out and walks away. It's a vicious cycle—one that sacrifices the many for the profits of the few.

Challenging the IP Fairy Tale: Time for Real Change

The insolvency industry likes to present itself as a white knight, galloping in to rescue creditors and bring order to chaos. In reality, they're more akin to scavengers, picking over the remains of failing businesses and extracting whatever profit they can before moving on to the next carcass. They are not protectors of the economy. They are opportunists, driven by fees and unchecked by meaningful regulation.

We need a system that recognises that failure is not the end of the road. Businesses can fail without their directors being treated like criminals. Employees deserve better than to be thrown on the scrap heap because it's expedient for an IP. Creditors deserve more than the crumbs left after fees have been extracted. A fair insolvency system would offer businesses a genuine chance at recovery and directors a fair shot at a second chance. It would understand that entrepreneurship requires risk, and it would protect the innovators, not penalise them.

The current system doesn't just need tweaking—it needs an overhaul. Until we confront the uncomfortable truths behind the insolvency industry, nothing will change. The IPs will continue to thrive, growing fat off the misery of others, while the rest of us pay the price. The economic stability they claim to provide is a fantasy; the truth is chaos wrapped in bureaucracy and sold with a smile. Until we are willing to challenge the myths, we will be left with a system that crushes dreams and penalises ambition, all in the name of short-term profit.

The Economic Toll: How the Insolvency Industry is Killing Growth in the UK

The insolvency industry in the UK, designed ostensibly to manage business failure responsibly, has instead become a machine that punishes entrepreneurship, discourages risk-taking, and ultimately throttles economic growth. By treating liquidation as a default solution, charging fees that would make even seasoned con artists blush, and making sure directors are scared stiff of trying again, the UK insolvency model creates an environment where failure is less of a learning experience and more of a scarlet letter. This chapter dissects how this deeply flawed system suffocates economic resilience, crushes innovation, and generally weakens the UK's prospects of staying competitive.

A System That Punishes Risk-Taking

Entrepreneurship is, by nature, risky. Risk-taking is what drives innovation, creates jobs, and fuels growth. But in the UK, entrepreneurship is treated as something reckless, like sticking a fork into an electrical socket. Entrepreneurs are encouraged to toe the line, and heaven help you if you actually want to do something bold. The insolvency system here doesn't just discourage failure; it turns it into a financial crucifixion. Directors know that when insolvency looms, they're facing disqualification, personal financial ruin, and possibly the equivalent of a financial colonoscopy over some forgotten lunch expenses. It's no wonder that the average director is more likely to bury their dreams than take another risk.

According to a recent survey by the British Chambers of Commerce, 42% of UK business owners say they hesitate to expand or innovate due to fear of insolvency consequences. Let that sink in: nearly half of the country's entrepreneurs are so afraid of the big, bad IPs that they won't even try. Instead of encouraging people to push boundaries, the system tells them to sit quietly, mind their margins, and hope the wolves don't show up. And that's hardly the entrepreneurial spirit needed for a thriving economy, is it?

The Liquidation-Driven Model: Destroying Value and Jobs

The UK's insolvency model seems to have a particular fondness for liquidation—a love affair that's been devastating for the wider economy. Instead of exploring restructuring, recovery, or even just stalling to catch a breath, IPs see liquidation as the simplest, most lucrative option. And why wouldn't they? It's fast, it's easy, and it pays handsomely. Whether it's best for the business, the employees, or the economy at large is very much an afterthought—if it's thought about at all.

The consequences of this liquidation fixation are severe. We're not just talking about a few businesses going belly up; we're talking about thousands of jobs vaporising in the blink of an eye. In 2022, over 200,000 jobs disappeared due to company liquidations. That's not just a statistic; it's a giant flashing sign that says, "We'd rather burn it all down than try to save it." For every job lost, there's a family facing financial instability and a government picking up the slack with welfare payments. It's as if the entire system is more invested in feeding the IPs than keeping people employed. What a vision for economic growth—draining value straight from the source while the taxpayer holds the bag.

The Ripple Effect: Wrecking Supply Chains and Local Economies

When a business goes into liquidation, it's not just that business that suffers—it's the suppliers, the customers, the employees, the local chippy. It's everyone who ever relied on that company, right down to the bloke who delivers the sandwiches. The ripple effect is like dropping a massive stone in a small pond: the waves don't just hit one entity; they keep spreading until everyone is soaked in misery. The insolvency industry's fixation on liquidation, on taking the path of least resistance, exacerbates these ripple effects and leaves entire supply chains shattered.

When a manufacturing firm gets pushed into liquidation, their unpaid invoices push their suppliers towards insolvency. Suddenly, a couple of missed payments up the chain and you've got a financial chain reaction that could obliterate half a dozen businesses. It's like watching dominoes fall, except instead of satisfying clicks, it's the sound of livelihoods collapsing and skills disappearing from local communities forever. Talk about economic resilience—more like economic fragility, lovingly nurtured by the UK's favourite fee-driven industry.

The Chilling Effect on New Business Formation

Not only does the system scare established businesses away from risk, but it also discourages would-be entrepreneurs from even entering the fray. Why start something new when you know that one misstep could lead to financial ruin, a public flogging disguised as an "insolvency process," and the distinct possibility that you'll be too broke to ever try again? This chilling effect ensures that the UK's long-term competitive prospects are slowly eroding, while other nations welcome risk-takers with open arms and safety nets.

According to the UK Business Start-Up Survey, new business registrations have plummeted by 15% over the last five years. That's a 15% reduction in dreamers willing to take the plunge—because they've heard the horror stories of what happens when things go wrong. It's as if the whole country is collectively deciding that entrepreneurship is for suckers. Who needs fresh ideas and new ventures, anyway? Not the UK, apparently—we'll just keep squeezing the juice out of whatever husks remain until the economy is as dry as an IP's empathy.

Innovation? Not Under This Regime

If you want innovation, you need people willing to take risks—and if you want people to take risks, you have to make sure that the penalties for failure aren't utterly life-destroying. The UK's insolvency system ensures that every would-be innovator knows exactly what happens if their big idea doesn't pan out: a humiliating autopsy of their finances, IPs breathing down their neck, and potentially years of financial struggle, as their personal assets are raided to satisfy whatever fees can't be squeezed from the carcass of the business.

No wonder, then, that we're trailing in innovation. The UK ranks a measly 13th on the Global Innovation Index—trailing behind the United States, Germany, and even Sweden. Over a third of UK business leaders admit they're reluctant to invest in new technologies or expand into uncharted waters, all because of the fear that the insolvency industry will have their heads if things go wrong. The UK isn't losing out to international competition because we lack talent or ideas; we're losing because the system punishes anyone who dares to try and change things.

The Impact on Investment: Who Would Bother?

In a global economy, investment is king. Investors look for places where they can put their money into ventures with real growth potential—and that means environments that support recovery, not just failure. The UK's insolvency system, with its liquidation-first, profits-for-the-practitioners approach, makes the country look about as attractive to investors as a burning skip.

Foreign direct investment (FDI) in the UK has plummeted by over 10% from 2019 to 2022. It's hardly a mystery why: investors aren't exactly queuing up to pour their money into a place where any stumble means a business ends up in the greedy maw of an IP. It's like setting up a lemonade stand knowing the first rainy day means the taxman and half your neighbours will be by to strip your assets. Investors, unsurprisingly, prefer places where businesses are allowed to falter and then try again—not somewhere they're fed into the wood chipper at the first sign of trouble.

Productivity and Economic Growth: A Slow Suffocation

Productivity is a cornerstone of economic strength. The more efficiently an economy can produce, the better off everyone is. Yet, the UK has struggled with productivity for over a decade, and the insolvency model certainly hasn't helped. When businesses are prematurely liquidated, institutional knowledge is lost, jobs disappear, and potential growth is destroyed before it even has a chance to get going. It's economic euthanasia—pulling the plug on companies before the doctors have even tried CPR.

The Confederation of British Industry (CBI) reports that UK productivity is 16% lower than the G7 average. That's billions lost every year in wasted potential—and the insolvency system plays a starring role in this national tragedy. Instead of helping companies recover, innovate, and grow, the system gleefully dismantles them, making sure no stone is left unturned and no fee is left uncollected. It's not just short-term growth we're sacrificing; it's the long-term prosperity of an entire country.

The Long-Term Consequences: Punishing the Risk-Takers, Stifling the Future

The knock-on effects of a punitive insolvency system extend far beyond a few failed companies. Over time, the UK's reputation as a place where entrepreneurship can thrive is eroded. Instead of being a nation that celebrates resilience and growth, we're becoming a cautionary tale—the place where risk-takers go to get ground into dust. This, in turn, discourages not only home-grown talent but also foreign entrepreneurs who might consider relocating here. Why would they? They've seen how the UK rewards those who dare to take risks—with a swift kick into liquidation and a multi-year stint paying off IP fees.

Countries that support risk-takers tend to reap the rewards: more innovation, more businesses, more jobs. The UK, on the other hand, seems intent on punishing failure so thoroughly that nobody in their right mind would ever want to try again. Unless we rethink this outdated, draconian insolvency approach, the UK will continue to lose its competitive edge—one failed, overly penalised business at a time.

A Call for Economic Reform

The UK's insolvency system is doing more than just managing business failures. It's actively undermining the country's economic health. By punishing risk, favouring liquidation over any attempt at recovery, and scaring away potential entrepreneurs, it's draining the life out of the UK's economic prospects. It's high time we shifted towards a model that actually supports recovery, allows directors to fail without having their entire lives ruined, and creates an environment where innovation and growth can flourish.

The next chapter will examine how the insolvency process destroys the personal and family lives of those unfortunate enough to end up in its web.

The Personal Toll of Predatory Liquidations

Insolvency practitioners love to talk about the efficiency of their processes, the professionalism of their investigations, and their so-called dedication to "creditor recovery." What they don't mention—what they can't mention—is the human wreckage they leave in their wake. Behind the jargon and the cold efficiency lies a devastating truth: predatory liquidations don't just dismantle businesses; they destroy lives. Families are fractured, individuals spiral into depression, and the collective trust in society erodes. I've seen this toll firsthand, and it's a dark, grim picture of what happens when an industry prioritises profit over humanity.

The Family Unit: Collateral Damage in a System of Profit

When a director is dragged through a predatory liquidation, the family often suffers even more than the individual. A director under relentless scrutiny from insolvency practitioners isn't just dealing with business failure—they're dealing with personal annihilation. I've spoken to directors who've been hounded for years over so-called "misfeasance," their every decision combed through with the benefit of hindsight. This isn't justice; it's legalised harassment.

Imagine what that does to a family. Children, particularly young ones, see their parent go from a confident, hardworking business leader to a shadow of themselves. The stress is inescapable, and for children, it's formative. A once-stable home becomes a battleground of financial stress, sleepless nights, and simmering resentment. Spouses struggle to keep the family afloat, often taking on extra work or stretching themselves emotionally thin to support their partner. I've seen marriages fall apart under the strain of endless investigations, and when the family unit collapses, it ripples through generations.

The long-term effects on children are profound. With a parent under constant pressure, their future prospects dim. They might lose their home, their sense of stability, even their trust in authority. What kind of society allows its brightest, most ambitious citizens to be reduced to this? And what kind of message does that send to their children? Don't try. Don't build. Don't take risks—because the system will crush you.

The Aggressiveness of the Takedown: From Depression to Despair

The insolvency industry's aggressive tactics don't just ruin finances; they obliterate self-worth. It's David versus Goliath, except David isn't armed with a sling—he's tied up with red tape while Goliath charges a £400 hourly fee to dismantle his life. The process is deliberately isolating. Directors are treated as villains, questioned relentlessly, and stripped of the dignity they once had as business leaders. For many, it's the first time in their lives they feel powerless.

Depression sets in fast. And I don't mean the kind you can walk off. I mean the kind that makes people question the point of getting out of bed. The kind that makes a father or mother start to wonder if their family would be better off without them. It's not hyperbole—it's reality. I've personally known multiple directors who couldn't take it anymore. The constant letters, the accusations, the clawback demands that feel more like extortion than justice—it broke them. They ended their lives because the system didn't just take their business; it took their hope.

The ripple effect of these suicides is staggering. Families are left in emotional and financial ruin. Friends and colleagues carry the guilt of not being able to intervene. And society as a whole pays the price. The NHS picks up the tab for the mental health fallout, overwhelmed as it is. Local councils step in to deal with housing crises for widows and orphaned children. And yet, the insolvency industry carries on, undeterred, churning through directors like they're just numbers on a spreadsheet.

A Society of the Broken and Distrusting

The damage doesn't stop with the individual or their family. Predatory liquidations create a society of embittered, broken people. Directors who've been through the system often emerge distrustful of everyone: government, accountants, lawyers, and even their peers. They've been burned so badly that the idea of starting over feels impossible. The bitterness isn't just personal—it spreads. These directors become vocal critics, warning others against entrepreneurship, creating a chilling effect that discourages risk-taking and innovation.

This erosion of trust has wider consequences. Communities lose their glue when directors and small businesses vanish. Employees who lose jobs during insolvencies are less likely to trust future employers. Customers become sceptical of local businesses, unsure if they'll even last the year. And as more people experience the fallout of predatory liquidations—either directly or through someone they know—the collective morale of society takes a hit.

What's worse is that the system fosters cynicism. Directors who survive often feel they have to game the system themselves just to get by. Instead of fostering innovation, the UK is fostering a generation of people who believe the only way to win is to cheat, cut corners, or stay small and invisible. That's not a recipe for a thriving economy—it's a death spiral.

A System That Chooses Profit Over People

What's truly galling is that all of this—the broken families, the suicides, the societal distrust—stems from one thing: the insolvency industry's relentless pursuit of profit. Insolvency practitioners don't see directors as people; they see them as opportunities. An investigation isn't about justice—it's about billable hours. A clawback demand isn't about fairness—it's about padding the balance sheet.

I've sat across from directors who broke down in tears, telling me how they'd given everything to their business, only to be treated like criminals. These aren't villains. They're the backbone of the economy, the people who create jobs, pay taxes, and build communities. And yet, the system treats them as disposable, chasing short-term gains at the expense of the long-term health of the UK.

It doesn't have to be this way. There's nothing inevitable about this level of destruction. But until the insolvency industry is held accountable—until its profit motives are stripped away—this cycle of devastation will continue.

In the next chapter, we will look at how other countries have modernised their insolvency systems to encourage resilience, innovation, and economic prosperity—providing a roadmap for how the UK could stop shooting itself in the foot and start fostering an environment where failure is a step on the path to success, not the end of the line.

A Global Comparison – How the Insolvency System in the UK Stacks Up Against the US and Europe

The insolvency industry in the UK proudly declares itself the gatekeeper of orderly business shutdowns, a kind of grim bureaucratic priesthood managing the last rites for dying enterprises. Yet across the pond in the United States, they do things a little differently. Imagine a world where the winding down of a business doesn't require forking over a pound of flesh to an insolvency practitioner (IP), where directors can exit the scene without having their pockets emptied and their reputations dragged through the mud. Sounds like a fantasy? Well, it's just everyday business across the Atlantic.

In this chapter, we'll pull back the curtain on how the US, Germany, and the Netherlands handle business closures without relying on the IP cabal, and how their flexibility provides them with a competitive edge. Meanwhile, back in the UK, the IPs are holding a liquidation bonanza—director dignity be damned.

The United States: Winding Down Without Mandatory IP Involvement

The US insolvency model is everything the UK's system is not—namely, humane and logical. Over there, business closure doesn't automatically involve dragging an IP into the mix like a vampire summoned to drain the last drop. Instead, directors are trusted—yes, trusted—to wind down voluntarily, preserving whatever remains without needing to pay for the privilege of being robbed blind by an IP.

How Voluntary Winding Down Works in the US

In the United States, when the chips are down, directors can choose "voluntary dissolution," which is just a fancy way of saying, "Let's not make this worse than it already is." Directors can directly negotiate with creditors, sell off assets, and distribute remaining funds—all without paying an IP to sit there with a meter running.

Take, for instance, a small US manufacturing company running out of steam due to supply chain issues. In the US, the directors can simply decide to pack it in, settle debts, sell assets, and call it a day. They don't need to hire an IP to put on a show, pretend they care, and send a hefty bill for the performance.

Statistics on Voluntary Dissolution and Business Flexibility

According to data from the US Small Business Administration, over 70% of small businesses that close each year do so without ever sniffing formal insolvency proceedings. Directors get to do their thing without the white-knuckle anxiety of IP-induced financial surgery, which preserves dignity, minimises fees, and prevents the emotional scarring so many UK directors endure.

This trust in directors' competence is something the UK can't seem to get its head around. Instead, it's as though the entire country collectively decided that anyone whose business folds must clearly be a dunce who can't be trusted with the process. Enter the IP—the "expert" with their ledger, ready to plunder whatever is left.

Why the US System Benefits Entrepreneurs and the Economy

This director-led dissolution model helps entrepreneurs pick themselves up, dust off, and have another go. In one case, a small US restaurant chain was able to dissolve voluntarily and pay off creditors in full—all without the prying hands of an IP reaching into the till. Imagine that. And the directors? Free to start their next venture without the dark cloud of UK-style insolvency hanging over their heads. They weren't condemned to spend the next decade explaining themselves to every potential investor who looked at their CV.

The UK's Contrasting Model: IP-Driven Winding Down

In the UK, every failing business must appoint an IP—no exceptions, no grace. It's like insisting on a hangman at every funeral, just to make sure no one gets up again. The moment a company hits troubled waters, an IP must be brought in to "help"—though help usually means siphoning off whatever's left.

The Financial and Personal Toll on Directors

Appointing an IP isn't just an obligation; it's an exercise in masochism. The Insolvency Service reports that IP fees routinely eat up between 20% and 40% of a company's assets, a fat slice considering that creditors are left gnawing on scraps. One UK retail business entered insolvency with a healthy £1 million in assets; after the IP's fee-fest, creditors received barely enough to buy a good lunch.

And if you think directors get out unscathed, think again. UK directors are subjected to intense scrutiny, potential disqualification, and threats of personal bankruptcy—all so the IP can comb through every decision they've ever made, like a forensic archaeologist digging for excuses to bill more hours.

Germany and the Netherlands: Alternatives to IP-Driven Closure

The UK's insistence on IP-driven misery is increasingly out of sync with the rest of the world. Germany and the Netherlands have realised that maybe, just maybe, directors could handle winding down without needing an IP breathing down their necks and rifling through their bank accounts.

Germany's Director-Led Closure Options

Germany offers directors a "do-it-yourself" closure if they can prove that the creditors are getting their due without the circus of insolvency proceedings. Here, directors retain control, wind things down, and walk away with their pride intact—something that's near-impossible in the UK. Early intervention is encouraged in Germany, too—meaning directors are given the tools to fix issues before someone decides an IP should swoop in like a very expensive grim reaper.

The Netherlands' WHOA Model: A Balance of Control and Oversight

The Netherlands recently introduced the WHOA model, which is essentially "insolvency without all the nonsense." Directors negotiate directly with creditors and avoid insolvency altogether unless it's genuinely needed. It's almost as if the Dutch realised that punishing directors for trying is counterproductive. Crazy, right?

One Dutch hospitality group, battered by COVID, was able to use WHOA to negotiate an exit with creditors, close up shop, and—get this—retain relationships with creditors, all without being dragged through insolvency. Compare this to the UK, where creditors are usually left waiting for whatever loose change trickles out after the IP's bill.

How the UK's IP-Driven Model Creates a Competitive Disadvantage

Mandatory IP involvement is like strapping a concrete block to a drowning swimmer—it guarantees the outcome. The UK is effectively telling directors that failure isn't just a possibility—it's a lifelong sentence. If your business struggles, expect to be financially drained and personally scrutinised, all while the IP collects their handsome fee.

Economic Impact of IP-Driven Processes on the Broader UK Economy

IPs, on average, take home more than 20% of estate value in fees. That's 20% that could have gone to creditors but instead disappears into the administrative ether. And it's not just the numbers that sting; it's the effect this model has on risk-taking in the UK. Entrepreneurs look at the risks and ask themselves if it's really worth it. For 40% of them, the answer is no. Compare that with the US, where directors aren't constantly bracing for the IP-axeman, and it's easy to see why entrepreneurship flourishes over there.

The Need for Reform to Foster Economic Resilience

Germany, the Netherlands, and the US all trust directors to wind down responsibly. By contrast, the UK presumes incompetence, ropes in the IPs, and lets them dine at the estate's expense. Reform is urgently needed if the UK wants to maintain any semblance of competitiveness. The country should allow voluntary dissolutions, director-led closures, or minimally-supervised processes, much like the WHOA model. Anything less is just inviting the continued slow death of UK entrepreneurship.

Conclusion: Learning From the World

The world isn't waiting for the UK to catch up. Across the US and Europe, directors are winding down companies without IPs siphoning off the spoils. They're leaving without a noose of debt around their neck, with the potential to rebuild and innovate, instead of being consigned to financial purgatory.

If the UK wants to nurture entrepreneurship and innovation, it needs to fundamentally rethink its approach to insolvency. Let directors do their own dirty work. Let them talk to their creditors, sell their assets, and close up shop without IPs treating every failure as a personal fee farm. If the UK can do that, perhaps it can reclaim its reputation as a centre of entrepreneurial spirit, rather than a land where, once you've fallen, the system's only interest is in seeing how much more you can bleed.

In the next chapter, we'll explore specific reforms that could dismantle the UK's current punitive insolvency framework and replace it with a fairer, recovery-focused model—one that finally aligns with the principles of entrepreneurship, resilience, and dignity. Because until then, every risk in the UK will feel like walking a tightrope above a pit full of IPs, all sharpening their knives, waiting for you to slip.

The Struggle for Reform and the Resistance to Change

The 1986 Insolvency Act was a defining moment in UK insolvency law—and not in a good way. It fundamentally altered the landscape by privatising the process and birthing an industry focused on making profits off failing businesses. The Act was pitched as a move towards efficiency, a clean break from cumbersome bureaucracy to sleek private management. But what really happened was more akin to getting Felix the cat to guard the fish market. They handed the keys to the treasury to private insolvency practitioners (IPs), who, unsurprisingly, took the opportunity to enrich themselves. Public oversight was stripped away, and an industry designed to suck value out of struggling companies was born.

I have seen it firsthand: the moment a company enters insolvency, IPs swoop in like vultures, picking apart whatever remains. They maximise their fees, often with little regard for genuine recovery or the fate of the business. And why wouldn't they? The system was set up to incentivise precisely this kind of predatory behaviour. The directors and creditors are merely characters in the background of the IP's show—extras who are dragged along for the ride, powerless as they watch their companies devoured.

The 1986 Act introduced an entirely new class of professionals—insolvency practitioners—paid directly by the cases they managed. Unlike civil servants who might have had some sense of duty to the public, these practitioners were given near-total control over proceedings. They set their fees. They managed the process. And they did it all with minimal oversight. This wasn't just a reform; it was the birth of an empire, one in which IPs reigned supreme and unchecked.

This self-serving model wasn't hard to predict. Put people in a position where they can profit off the misfortune of others without meaningful checks and balances, and you get precisely what we've seen. Throughout my career advising distressed companies, I've worked with countless directors who thought entering insolvency was the first step towards recovery, only to discover it was a shortcut to ruin. IPs drained their assets, charged through the nose, and left nothing behind for creditors, much less for any semblance of business survival. The priority became about billing hours, not saving jobs or value—and why would it be anything else when the system had been architected that way?

By 2002, public discontent was becoming hard to ignore. The government responded with the Enterprise Act, waving around promises of creating a "rescue culture." Sounds great, right? They said they wanted to make administration, rather than liquidation, the default route for companies in trouble. The plan was to preserve jobs and keep businesses afloat. Enter the concept of "pre-packs," the so-called silver bullet allowing companies to sell their assets in advance of formal insolvency. The marketing was there—it was supposed to be about giving companies a fighting chance, allowing them to keep operating while shedding the dead weight.

But what really happened? The Enterprise Act, much like its predecessor, quickly became a convenient vehicle for IPs to do what they do best—extract fees. Pre-packs, instead of being the lifeline for struggling companies, became another tool for IPs to wrap things up quickly, sell off the assets, and get paid—preferably in full, and preferably before anyone else even knew what hit them. This was a "rescue culture" in name only, a narrative to keep the critics at bay while IPs quietly continued their liquidation-first practices. I've seen pre-packs used to shuffle assets between related companies at lightning speed, only for the remainder to be liquidated—nothing more than a thinly disguised fire sale with a pretty name. If the Enterprise Act was meant to change the incentives driving IPs, it failed spectacularly.

Fast forward to 2015, and we had the Small Business, Enterprise and Employment Act—another piece of legislation introduced amidst growing public frustration. The goal this time was transparency. They said IP fees had gotten out of control, and Parliament was going to do something about it. The Act promised creditors more rights to challenge IP fees. They could take action if fees were abusive or egregious. Except, there's a catch—or ten. Because in practice, the system was rigged from the outset. The 2015 Act was like handing someone a slingshot and asking them to take down a tank. Sure, creditors could challenge IP fees, but good luck finding a lawyer willing to take on the case without charging you a fortune—and by the end of it, even if you won, you'd be in deeper financial trouble than you started.

I've seen this over and over. Clients come to me bewildered by the numbers on their insolvency paperwork, seeing six-figure fees for what's essentially asset-stripping with a side of administration. Yet when they try to push back, they're hit with mountains of procedural red tape and costs that effectively make any challenge pointless. The right to challenge might exist on paper, but in reality, it's a joke—a paper tiger. Meanwhile, IPs keep setting fees to whatever they please, and who's going to stop them? Certainly not a bunch of creditors who are already out of pocket and disempowered by the very system they're supposed to be protected by.

What's remarkable—and by remarkable, I mean infuriating—is how resistant IPs have been to any form of meaningful oversight or reform. Every time Parliament tries to introduce fee caps or greater regulation, IPs lobby aggressively, leveraging their influence to maintain their position. They've cultivated an air of indispensability, arguing that they're the only ones with the expertise to handle complex insolvencies. And so, they fend off regulation, fee caps, and any attempt to curb their practices with the precision of a surgeon and the tenacity of a pit bull.

The IP industry argues that without them, insolvencies would descend into chaos—that they are the ones who maintain order and propriety in a financial crisis. This claim would be laughable if it weren't so tragic. I've seen plenty of "order": creditors left with mere pennies while IPs pocket hundreds of thousands, directors whose personal savings are bled dry to satisfy investigative fees that ultimately lead nowhere. I've seen employees who could have been spared thrown out like yesterday's trash because liquidation—the quick and easy option—was chosen over trying to keep a business running.

The cumulative effect of these so-called "reforms"—the Insolvency Act of 1986, the Enterprise Act of 2002, and the Small Business Act of 2015—is a system where insolvency practitioners operate without real checks or balances. They're like medieval lords, collecting fees with impunity while those around them are left to starve. Each time we've had a shot at reform, we've blown it. And let's be honest: it's not because we lack the will; it's because IPs and their allies in the corridors of power have been too successful at lobbying, blocking, and obfuscating.

So, here we are—in a system where IPs continue to set their own rules, pocket outrageous fees, and get away with it because there's no real accountability. They are effectively self-regulating monopolists, and anyone who's ever had to deal with an IP knows exactly how much regard they have for fairness. In my years of advising distressed businesses, I've seen directors walk into the insolvency process full of hope, believing that they might be able to restructure, save jobs, and pull through. Instead, they're quickly disabused of that notion, finding themselves up against an IP with one agenda—maximise fees, liquidate the assets, move on to the next one.

True reform requires a complete rethink. Transparency, by itself, is worthless. We need enforceable limits—caps on IP fees that aren't just theoretical but binding. We need government oversight that isn't riddled with loopholes or left toothless by industry lobbying. Most importantly, we need a genuine commitment to recovery—an insolvency system that works to keep businesses afloat rather than dismantling them at the first sign of trouble. IPs have had their chance, and they've proven that, left unchecked, they'll act in their own interest every time.

Instead of IPs charging whatever they like, a government body should provide fixed-fee insolvency services. Imagine if directors were given the tools and breathing room to attempt recovery first, rather than being funnelled straight into liquidation. Imagine if creditors actually had a real voice, rather than being treated as afterthoughts once the IP has had their fill. None of this is pie in the sky—these are reforms that other countries have implemented with success. The only reason it hasn't happened here is because it's not in the interest of IPs or the powerful lobbying groups that protect them.

The UK's current insolvency system is a profit machine. It serves IPs and leaves everyone else—directors, creditors, employees—in the dust. The idea that insolvency is about providing a fair resolution is laughable. It's about monetising failure, ensuring that the people who are already down get pushed a little further. If we're serious about change—if we're serious about creating an insolvency system that serves the public interest—then we need to put an end to this charade of self-regulation and start putting in place real, enforceable checks. Until then, IPs will keep feeding at the trough, while everyone else just gets to watch as their livelihoods and investments are stripped for parts.

Right, all very well and good – but how should we fix it? What should the system really look like? Luckily, I've thought about that.

NEXT!

Rethinking the Insolvency System for Small and Medium Businesses

The UK's insolvency framework, with its heavy reliance on insolvency practitioners (IPs), has proven to be a bureaucratic nightmare—expensive, punitive, and economically short-sighted. The system is designed to kick you while you're already down, then charging you for the boot. This is the reality faced by small and medium enterprises (SMEs) in the UK: a process where liquidation is the default setting, IPs profit handsomely off the remains, and struggling business owners are left questioning why they ever tried in the first place. If the goal was to make entrepreneurship as risky and joyless as possible, it's safe to say they've succeeded. But we've been over all this in depth, so what's the solution?

The time has come to rethink this insolvency hellscape, starting with minimising or even eliminating the role of IPs in winding down most SMEs. To foster a healthier, more resilient business environment, we need to swap out the vultures for real reform—a system that allows directors to take charge, preserves economic value, and eliminates unnecessary fees and punitive measures.

Director-Led Winding Down for SMEs

Let's start with a radical concept: what if directors were allowed to wind down their businesses themselves, without an IP breathing down their necks, racking up fees for the "service" of auctioning off the office kettle? In the UK, the moment a company hits the skids, an IP swoops in, supposedly to help. In reality, they're there to strip the copper wiring and charge you for the privilege. Directors should be allowed to retain control and close down their operations without this parasite attached to the process. The idea is simple—director-led, IP-free wind-downs for SMEs, allowing the people who built the business to also close it down in a dignified manner.

Under this model, directors would have the ability to negotiate directly with creditors, settle debts, and distribute any remaining assets without the need for an IP looking for any excuse to get paid. It's their business; they know it best, and they can certainly manage its end without someone pocketing 30% of the leftovers for "administrative expenses"—otherwise known as signing a few forms and making phone calls that cost £200 an hour.

Without IPs taking their slice, this director-led model would reduce costs dramatically, preserve more value for creditors, and allow directors to wind down without being treated like criminals. Better yet, it would restore some sense of dignity to business closure—a "farewell and goodnight" rather than the IP's "who gets the last laugh".

Introducing a Voluntary Settlement Pathway

Next, we need to talk about how the system could actually prevent insolvency before it happens. It's radical, I know—a system that stops things getting worse, instead of kicking directors into the financial abyss and handing them an IP-branded shovel for good measure. This brings us to the voluntary settlement pathway, where directors get the chance to collaborate with creditors early, reach repayment agreements, and generally avoid plunging into the abyss.

Imagine a world where, at the first sign of trouble, a director doesn't need to fear an IP's dark gaze but instead is offered a mediator to assist in finding a solution. Not a hunter, but a facilitator—someone there to help negotiate reasonable repayment terms with creditors instead of seeking out assets to liquefy. This model takes the emphasis away from blame and liquidation, and shifts it towards preserving jobs, business relationships, and value—all the good stuff that IPs find inconvenient to mention when they're eyeing their next payday.

In this world, liquidation isn't the default option; it's the last resort. And for once, creditors might get something close to a fair return, rather than the breadcrumbs IPs leave behind after consuming the lion's share in "administrative fees". The focus is on saving the ship, not ensuring the rats get a five-star meal before abandoning it.

Fee Caps and Real Transparency for IPs

If we're stuck with IPs in some cases—because, unfortunately, like a bad cold they just won't go away—then let's at least make sure they don't loot the joint in broad daylight. The introduction of fee caps and mandatory transparency would at least force IPs to take a smaller bite out of whatever's left.

IPs should have to justify their fees in detail, itemising every charge. Maybe then we'd see how absurd it is to bill thousands for "preparing documents", when the reality is probably closer to "printed off a template and made a cup of tea". With enforceable limits, IPs would have to think twice before billing a drowning company for a designer lifeboat, complete with branded oars. Caps on fees would ensure that some of what's left actually goes to creditors and not to the people supposedly "saving" the company.

The National Insolvency Ombudsman: A Concept So Obvious It Hurts

Then there's accountability—another concept the insolvency industry avoids like a plague. Enter the idea of a National Insolvency Ombudsman, whose sole purpose would be to investigate complaints, arbitrate disputes, and generally give IPs a reason to behave like half-decent human beings. Directors and creditors need somewhere to turn when the inevitable happens: the IP's fees start piling up, oversight goes out the window, and the entire process becomes indistinguishable from a high-stakes smash-and-grab.

An independent ombudsman could act as the thorn in the side of IPs, ensuring there's at least a modicum of fairness and transparency in the process. For once, directors wouldn't have to feel like they were playing a rigged game. IPs might actually find themselves answering questions—real, tough questions—about why it was necessary to charge £500 for making a phone call to confirm that, yes, there really are no more assets left to sell.

Early-Stage Rescue Programs: A Novel Idea Called "Helping"

The UK system has another glaring problem: support for businesses facing financial issues only kicks in when it's too late. It's like calling the fire brigade after the house has burned down and then wondering why the insurance company's rates are astronomical. We need more early-stage rescue programs—a kind of "let's sort this out before it turns into a full-blown catastrophe" scheme. We do our best to help everyone, but there's only so much we can take on.

In France, they've got something like this—a little thing called "Sauvegarde"—which aims to prevent businesses from going under by offering advisory services and creditor mediation at the first sign of trouble. It turns out that getting a bit of guidance early on can actually stop the inevitable march towards insolvency. Who knew? It's a model that doesn't just write off businesses at the first sign of distress; it's about prevention, not punishment.

UK businesses should be able to seek help before the IPs started rubbing their hands together in anticipation. We offer a service where directors can get advice on restructuring, financial management, and, crucially, creditor negotiation. This way, fewer businesses end up in the liquidation grinder, fewer employees lose their jobs, and fewer directors are left staring into the financial void.

Stop Treating Directors Like Criminals

Finally, we need to talk about the absurdity of mandatory investigations for directors of small businesses. Under the current model, every single director of an insolvent company gets treated like a potential criminal. Even if their only crime was trying to make payroll during a recession, they're slapped with scrutiny that, conveniently, comes with its own stack of IP-generated fees.

Let's stop pretending every failure involves wrongdoing. Instead, reserve investigations for cases where there's actual clear evidence of serious staring-you-in-the-face misconduct. If a small company goes under without anything suspicious, why on earth do we need an IP picking over the bones? Imagine being the director of a tiny café, unable to keep afloat during a pandemic, only to be called into question by someone billing £250 an hour to check if you spent too much on oat milk that one time. The current system doesn't prevent abuse; it prevents recovery and reinvention. It's time to let honest directors go, and let them go with their dignity intact.

Building a Fairer, Resilient Insolvency System

The UK's current insolvency system is a Frankenstein's monster of punitive measures, high costs, and misplaced priorities. Reforming it means rethinking who should be involved, when, and for how much. A director-led winding down process, a voluntary settlement pathway, an ombudsman, and early intervention—these aren't just ideas; they're necessary shifts towards a system that prioritises economic resilience over exploitation.

Because here's the thing: entrepreneurship is messy. Businesses fail. But those failures shouldn't be the end. They should be a chapter, not the final word. A reformed system would see insolvency as a chance to reset, not an opportunity to line the pockets of whoever got appointed to oversee the autopsy. And until we make that shift, the only people winning are the ones with "Insolvency Practitioner" on their office door—a door likely paid for, ironically, with someone else's misfortune.

In the next chapter, we'll look at how these changes could impact the broader economy—how reimagining the UK's insolvency system could lead to better recovery rates, more innovation, and a country that treats business risk not as something to be feared, but as something to be managed and, ultimately, rewarded.

Bloated Britian – The Other Factors

Britain is not just going backwards; it's willingly stepping off a cliff, comforted by the delusion that a cushy landing awaits below. For years, we've wrapped ourselves in layers of false security, with government spending like a never-ending comfort blanket, interest rates kept laughably low, and quantitative easing that's essentially been a financial smoke-and-mirrors trick. The end result? Nobody has any incentive to push forward, to innovate, to risk anything. Why would they, when doing nothing has become the most lucrative business model going? Buy a house, sit on it, and watch the value inflate like a balloon—it's that simple. And in the meantime, the rest of the economy rots, left to those foolish enough to try to actually *build* something.

Government spending has ballooned into something grotesque. Thirty years ago, government intervention was limited, something you turned to when all else failed. Today? It's baked into everything. The state has grown into this bloated leviathan—massive, sluggish, inefficient—trying to micromanage every facet of the economy. Back in the 1990s, government spending hovered around 35% of GDP. Fast forward to today, and we're well past 40%, creeping ever closer to half the economy being directly controlled or influenced by the state. That's not a mixed economy; that's a nanny state on steroids.

It's like we've forgotten that an economy isn't some charity project. It's not about keeping everyone comfortable, with government cash flowing to plaster over every crack. It's supposed to be driven by productivity, by people who put something on the line—their money, their time, their ideas—in hopes of building something worthwhile. But no. The state's endless spending spree has turned us all into passive dependents. Nobody wants to put skin in the game anymore because why bother when the government's always there to catch you, smoothing out the bumps, numbing the pain? The economy has become a no-risk zone where ambition goes to die.

And interest rates—let's talk about those. For years, they've been held artificially low. The Bank of England has been terrified of doing the one thing that could reintroduce a sense of value into money: make borrowing cost something. Saving has become a sucker's game. Why save when inflation's eating away at your returns and borrowing is practically free? This country's been high on cheap credit for over a decade, and now we're in the hangover phase, and it's ugly. The result of all this is that debt—personal, corporate, governmental—has ballooned to dangerous levels. But instead of facing the reality, we keep pumping the system with cheap money and hoping for the best.

And then there's the grand illusion of quantitative easing. QE was sold to us as a quick fix—a shot in the arm to get the economy moving during the financial crisis. But like that one party guest who won't leave, it's still here, quietly lurking in the background. What started as an emergency measure has become part of the furniture. The side effect? Asset prices—homes, equities, anything you can get your hands on—have shot through the roof. The problem is, the real economy hasn't kept up. It's not the entrepreneurs who've benefited; it's the asset owners. It's the folks who bought their house thirty years ago, who've done nothing but watch the value of their property soar while the rest of the country struggles to even afford a place to rent. It's a rigged game, and everyone's pretending that's just how it should be.

Owning a house has become the ultimate get-rich-quick scheme—not by building, not by contributing, but by simply *being there*. There's no real effort required, just ride the wave of government policy. And while everyone's busy counting the paper wealth of their bricks and mortar, where's the incentive to take a risk? Why would you? We've got a society that's become allergic to ambition. The path to success isn't hard work or taking a chance anymore; it's buying property and sitting on it. If you want to try something different—start a business, innovate, disrupt—you're a fool. Because everyone knows that the real money is in doing nothing.

The tragic thing is, we've made risk-taking almost impossible. Starting a business today is a minefield—between taxes, regulatory red tape, and a culture that's grown deeply suspicious of anyone trying to do something ambitious. We've glamorised safety, stability, and predictability, and we've demonised the very people who drive progress. If you're someone who wants to build, you're battling not just the natural obstacles of starting something new but a societal attitude that's more interested in where you live than what you do.

And let's not forget who's cheering on this sad state of affairs: the homeowners, the investors, the policy-makers. Everyone's complicit. The homeowner loves their inflated property value; the politician loves the easy votes that come with rising home equity; the investors love the predictability of a government-backed system that keeps the money flowing. The result? An economy that's stuck—immovable—propped up on bricks and mortar, with the government pumping cash into an increasingly fragile structure. And everyone's acting like it's all perfectly fine, as long as property prices keep rising.

But take a step back and look at what's actually happening. The UK is crumbling under its own weight—an economy addicted to asset bubbles and state intervention. We're infatuated with rising house prices as if that's a sign of progress. Meanwhile, the bits of the economy that actually require work—manufacturing, industry, entrepreneurship—are withering. People can't afford to start families because they can't afford a home; businesses are reluctant to invest because why bother when the return on capital is dwarfed by returns on property? The UK isn't just stagnating; it's actively digging itself deeper into a pit of dependency and complacency.

It's almost comical how we've shifted from a nation of builders and creators to a country obsessed with getting on the property ladder. At one point, Britain was the world's industrial leader, a place where people built things, created wealth, and made tangible contributions to the world. Now? We're a nation of landlords, cheerfully applauding our rising property values and hoping nothing changes too drastically.

We've traded ambition for assets, risk for rent, industry for inertia.

And that's the tragedy. We've demonised ambition because the biggest financial winners are the ones who've simply stayed put. The guy who bought a house in 1992 and did nothing but sit on it is lauded as savvy. Meanwhile, the person who tries to innovate, who dares to start something, who actually has the gall to build—they're the outliers, the fools for risking it all when everyone knows that buying bricks and waiting is the smarter move. When did we become a country that sees risk as a liability rather than a necessity?

It's not just the economy that's taken a hit—it's our culture. The values that once drove us—the spirit of enterprise, the willingness to put yourself on the line for something bigger—they're disappearing. And the result is a nation that's fundamentally fragile, ill-equipped to face the future because we've spent so long trying to insulate ourselves from every conceivable downside. We've mortgaged our future for the sake of comfort today, and we're running out of road.

We've also built a monster of a government—a bloated public sector that's almost double the size it was just three decades ago. This isn't just about hospitals and schools; it's about layers upon layers of bureaucracy, of departments and initiatives designed not to spark growth but to cushion us from every imaginable risk. It's about safety nets turned into hammocks, where the state's hand reaches into every aspect of our lives to shield us from the consequences of failure. And it's not sustainable. Not financially, not socially, not if we actually want to grow.

The irony is that in our quest to eliminate risk, we've made ourselves more vulnerable. We've turned the housing market into this untouchable golden goose, and now, anything that threatens to bring prices back to reality is seen as a crisis. But housing isn't supposed to be an investment strategy; it's supposed to be a place to live. The more we inflate that bubble, the more we price out the next generation, the ones who might actually want to do something other than sit on an asset and hope it makes them rich. We're failing them, and we're failing the future.

And then there's the insolvency system—a process that's supposed to help businesses bounce back but instead works to bury them under layers of administrative costs and punitive scrutiny. The insolvency process here is less about recovery and more about ensuring the vultures get fed first, with Insolvency Practitioners (IPs) circling any hint of weakness. It's a system that values extracting the last drop of blood over any meaningful attempt at recovery. How does that encourage anyone to take risks or start something new? Why would you bother, when you know the moment you falter, there's a queue ready to pick apart whatever's left?

How do we fix this mess? First, we need to admit we're in it. This isn't a temporary blip; it's a systemic collapse of ambition in favour of comfort. We need to start valuing risk again, seeing ambition as the force that moves us forward, not something to be discouraged. We need to create an environment where people actually want to build businesses, where starting a new venture is seen as something brave and valuable, not something reckless. And yes, that means taking a hard look at property prices, government spending, interest rates, and the bloated insolvency system—everything that's got us to this point.

We need policies that reward creation and innovation. It's time to get over our obsession with property and instead invest in people—in their ideas, in their willingness to take risks. The government needs to step back from trying to control every aspect of the economy, and instead create the conditions where real growth can happen. That means accepting that not every business will succeed, not every venture will pay off. And that's fine. Failure is part of the process; it's how we learn, adapt, and eventually succeed.

The truth is, without risk-takers, there's no future. Not an exciting one, anyway. We need to stop patting ourselves on the back for doing nothing and start celebrating the people who want to take a chance, who want to build. That's how we rebuild this country's economy—by backing those who are willing to put in the effort, who don't see their house as their life's greatest achievement, who aren't content with a society that rewards sitting still.

This chapter probably needed to be an entirely new book – watch this space - but I think it was necessary to paint the full picture of the current disaster we're in. Back to the topic at hand, how reforming the insolvency system should help.

Reviving British Industry and Entrepreneurial Spirit

Whilst there are a myriad of factors killing British entrepreneurial spirit, the UK's insolvency system has been the ultimate buzzkill for entrepreneurship. Think about it—instead of encouraging the creative mavericks who dare to dream, we've set up a system that waits eagerly to pounce the moment things don't go to plan. Imagine a tightrope walker setting out to cross a grand canyon, only to see a line of auditors ready to snip the rope the second it wobbles. We're here to change that narrative. To reinvent a system that doesn't just punish risk but celebrates it, supports it, and picks us up when we fall—preferably with a warm cup of tea and a hearty pat on the back.

Reforming our insolvency process isn't just about fixing a broken machine. No, it's about taking the spare parts and building something spectacular—something that honours our entrepreneurs, celebrates our innovators, and restores our rightful place as leaders in global enterprise. Let's be honest: the old ways haven't just worn out, they're taking up space in the loft alongside that exercise bike we never used. It's time for something fresh, bold, and just a little bit brave.

A Cultural Makeover: From Villains to Visionaries

We need a complete cultural reset here—a shift in how we see business failures. Because here's a crazy thought: What if we stopped treating our entrepreneurs like villains when their businesses don't pan out? I know—radical, right? Instead of throwing them into the bin marked "Failures," we could consider that maybe, just maybe, failure is a part of success. Take it from the likes of Edison or Branson—they'd be nothing without their setbacks. Let's treat our business founders as the brave, often slightly eccentric pioneers they are. Sure, maybe that organic piranha fish farm didn't quite catch on, but hey, at least they dared to dream!

Instead of obsessing over "What went wrong?", how about we start focusing on "What's next?" With our new reforms, we can give directors back the keys to their own businesses when things go sideways, rather than having some suited IP charging £300 an hour to pull apart what's left of their dreams. Let's move from doom and gloom to "You did your best, now what else can you do?" Let's keep the spirit of entrepreneurship alive and kicking—or at the very least, dusting itself off and getting back up again.

Innovation & Industry: Giving Back the Spark

A reformed insolvency system isn't just good for entrepreneurs—it's good for all of us. When business owners aren't scared stiff of total financial ruin, they might just be willing to take a few risks. You know, the kind of risks that lead to exciting new products, groundbreaking tech, and businesses that improve our quality of life (or at least give us fancier coffee machines). Imagine a future where startups and SMEs could actually focus on creating value without a constant fear of financial obliteration.

Imagine if our local butcher could try out that vegan sausage line without worrying that a bad month would end with a gaggle of IPs seizing his mincer. The reforms we've outlined—early intervention, voluntary settlements, director-led closures—are all about making space for businesses to breathe, experiment, and yes, occasionally screw up. But if they do? We've got a safety net instead of a meat grinder.

Firing Up Foreign Investment: Come One, Come All!

Now let's talk about how the world sees us. Spoiler alert: a lot of investors see the UK as the land where great ideas come to die in the jaws of insolvency. With our current rigid, liquidation-loving system, we've essentially put out a giant "Proceed With Caution" sign for international investors. Who in their right mind wants to pour cash into a system where one rough quarter means your assets are carted away by a smug administrator with too much hair gel?

If we truly want the UK to be a competitive player on the global stage, we need to make sure our businesses can not only survive the rough patches but come out stronger. By bringing in flexibility, early intervention, and some well-deserved compassion, we're essentially telling investors: "Hey, Britain's back. We've retired the Grim Reaper of business, and now we're all about growth and resilience."

Saving Jobs & Strengthening Local Economies: The Butterfly Effect

Here's the thing—every time a business goes under unnecessarily, it's not just directors and creditors who feel the hit. It's also the employees who lose their jobs, the suppliers who miss out on income, and even the local café that loses its best lunchtime customers. That ripple effect is what really kills communities, and if we're being honest, nobody likes a town full of shuttered windows and empty car parks.

Imagine if, instead of shutting up shop at the first sign of trouble, companies could actually get some support. Imagine a system that says: "Hey, how can we get you through this rough patch and out the other side?" Because when businesses stay open, people stay employed, communities stay vibrant, and local economies continue to hum along nicely. And maybe, just maybe, Gary from Accounts can still afford his Friday night curry—which, let's be honest, is really what it's all about.

Embracing the Glorious Art of Failing Better

The old insolvency system doesn't just fail businesses, it teaches entrepreneurs to fear failure itself. And that's tragic, because failure—done right—is the secret sauce of every great success story. We've all heard the tales of tech titans and inventors who bombed time and time again before finally nailing it. Imagine if, instead of being terrified of liquidation and all the unpleasantness that comes with it, directors knew that they'd have the opportunity to learn, pivot, and try again? No disgrace, no stigma—just a chance to fail better next time.

With our proposed changes, mandatory investigations and automatic director disqualifications for honest mistakes would be a thing of the past. Instead, we'd have a culture that says: "You know what, nice try. Here's how you can do better next time." We're not talking about coddling reckless behaviour—we're talking about creating an environment where calculated risk is rewarded, and where failure is a pit stop, not a dead end.

A New Dawn for British Business

Imagine a UK that is genuinely excited about entrepreneurship again—a place where people aren't constantly looking over their shoulders, worrying that the next stumble will cost them everything. Imagine a nation full of inventors, innovators, and dreamers who feel supported in taking the kind of risks that lead to amazing breakthroughs, knowing that their community and their country has their back.

It's not pie-in-the-sky stuff—it's the kind of future that's possible with just a few key changes to our outdated insolvency system. If we take out the fear, the stigma, and the vultures looking to cash in on every misstep, we'll find that British entrepreneurship is far from dead—it's just been waiting for a chance to shine.

Let this be our moment to embrace a new era for British business. To celebrate the brave souls who take a punt, who chase the big ideas, and who occasionally, spectacularly, crash and burn—only to get back up again. This is a call to action, to all of us—whether we're policymakers, business leaders, or just people who want to see our communities thrive—to demand a system that supports, rather than punishes, our risk-takers.

With these changes, we can turn the UK into a land of possibility once more—a place where every entrepreneur, every dreamer, knows that their journey, no matter the outcome, is something worth celebrating.

Bonus Chapter

Director's Survival Guide

If your business is facing tough times, know this: insolvency is not the answer—at least not yet. When things go south, the temptation to hand the reins to someone who promises to "fix it" can be powerful. But that's the bait that drags thousands of directors into formal insolvency every year. I've seen it too many times: directors cornered, frightened, pushed into insolvency by those who profit most from it, told that this is the only way out.

But your business isn't some hopeless case to put out of its misery. Think of it like a family member who's fallen on hard times. You wouldn't push them toward the door or "euthanise" them just because they're in a bad spot. Businesses are resilient, and with the right strategies, even a distressed one can claw its way back from the brink. This chapter outlines hard-won tactics to keep your company breathing, keep creditors at bay, and keep insolvency off the table.

Find a Buyer Before You Even Think About Insolvency

One of the most powerful and least discussed options for a struggling business is a distressed sale. Too many directors assume that because the company's balance sheet looks bleak, nobody would want to buy it. That's nonsense. There are investors, competitors, even employees who may see the potential in your business that you can't see from the trenches. Selling the company, even at a fraction of its value, can be a lifeline. It not only allows you to walk away with a degree of dignity but also lets the business itself continue under new ownership, preserving jobs and assets without the scorched-earth aftermath of insolvency.

I've had directors tell me, "But who would want to buy it?" And yet, time and again, I've seen distressed businesses snapped up by opportunists or competitors who saw a strategic angle. One director I worked with was knee-deep in debt, drowning in creditor demands, and fully convinced his only option was to shut down. We found a buyer who was more than willing to take over and breathe new life into the operation, freeing the director from endless obligations and letting the business itself survive. There's often a buyer out there—you just need to look before you let an IP have their way.

Watch Your Language: Don't Ever Use the Word "Insolvent"

Language matters, especially in a situation as sensitive as a company in trouble. Using the word "insolvent" is like ringing the dinner bell for insolvency practitioners, creditors, and every lurking legal eagle who'd love nothing more than to pick over the bones of your business. Once you admit to insolvency, even casually, the wheels of legal obligation start turning, and suddenly you're on a tightrope. Your duty shifts toward the creditors, and you're bound by law to protect their interests above all else. In other words, you're on a one-way track to liquidation.

Instead, keep your language neutral. You're facing challenges. You're exploring options. But avoid saying "insolvent" or "bankrupt" like the plague. I've seen directors throw that word around too soon and pay the price, trapped by their own admission. Keep your focus on solutions—distressed sales, restructuring, emergency financing—anything that keeps the lights on and the doors open. This way, you retain control and keep a flicker of hope alive for recovery.

Insolvency Practitioners Will Always Push for Formal Insolvency

When you're in deep water, there's a parade of so-called "experts" ready to throw you a lifeline—at a price. Insolvency practitioners are notorious for presenting formal insolvency as the only option, turning every situation into one that requires their "services." It's a hammer-and-nail mentality: every problem looks like a nail, and insolvency is the hammer. What's worse, they'll make it seem like the end is nigh unless you act immediately, pressuring you into liquidation or administration before you've had a chance to explore real alternatives.

Remember, formal insolvency isn't about saving your business; it's about a profit model. IPs don't get paid by finding ways to help you keep the company. They get paid by dismantling it. I once worked with a director who was dragged into a CVL by an IP's scare tactics. He'd been warned of impending doom, told there was no other choice, only to find out later that with a little breathing room, he could have stabilised the business and avoided liquidation entirely. If an IP starts talking like there's no other option, take that as your cue to run the other way.

Prioritise Yourself: Don't Drain Your Personal Finances Trying to Save the Company

One of the biggest mistakes directors make in times of distress is sacrificing their own financial stability for the business. The sentiment is noble—covering payroll from personal funds, trying to hold on to staff, paying down creditors out of your own pocket. But this isn't about nobility. If you're facing serious trouble, your first duty is to yourself and your financial well-being. Draining your savings, putting your personal assets on the line, and jeopardising your family's future to save a sinking ship will do nothing but create more pain in the long run.

I've seen directors go down with the ship, burned out and broke, clinging to some ideal that they're doing the "right thing." Trust me, your employees won't be singing your praises when you can't make payroll next month. And creditors? They'll still be knocking on your door, oblivious to your sacrifices. Let staff go sooner rather than later if it's inevitable, giving them the dignity of a clear exit. If you're hanging on just to keep paying wages, you're doing no one a favour, least of all yourself. Your own financial stability is paramount, and safeguarding it is a responsible choice, not a selfish one.

Take Control of Personal Guarantees Now, Not Later

Personal guarantees (PGs) are a nasty piece of business. When a company goes under, the PGs don't vanish. They stick to you, binding you personally to debts that should belong to the company. Too often, directors wait until they're in full crisis mode before dealing with PGs, hoping they'll somehow disappear in the chaos of insolvency. But these debts won't just go away—they'll be enforced, and you'll be left holding the bag if you don't handle them early.

I've seen directors who ignored their PGs until the end, only to find themselves with a string of personal liabilities that turned their lives upside down. If your business is on shaky ground, tackle PG'd debt first. It may mean prioritising these debts over others, but in a crisis, survival instincts should kick in. Forget "preferential creditors" if you're up against PG enforcement—the personal stakes are simply too high. Addressing PGs early keeps your personal exposure in check and gives you a shot at walking away intact.

Dispute Every Debt

When creditors start closing in, disputing debts is one of the simplest ways to buy time. A disputed debt can't be turned into a winding-up petition, statutory demand, or court order without a lengthy legal process. In my experience, disputing even minor debts can create a buffer that allows directors to regroup and plot a way forward without the immediate threat of creditors hammering on the door.

I've had directors who, under heavy creditor pressure, disputed every debt they could on any plausible grounds. It's not about evasion; it's about creating breathing room. By questioning amounts, contesting timelines, or challenging interpretations of invoices, you force creditors into a slower, more cautious process. Most creditors won't go through the trouble of a court case if they think they'll eventually get paid. Disputing debts can buy you months—a critical period to assess options and stabilise.

Relocate Your Registered Office

Changing your registered office might seem minor, but it's a simple step that makes a huge difference. When creditors start showing up unannounced, it disrupts the business, demoralises staff, and ramps up the pressure on directors. Moving your registered address to a city centre location shields you from these unwanted visits, keeping day-to-day operations focused and reducing the anxiety of confrontational creditor encounters.

I've seen directors who let their business address double as their home address, only to regret it when creditors turned up at their doorstep. Companies House allows directors to change their registered office location easily, and it's one of the best moves you can make to protect your privacy. Removing your home address from the public record is also worth considering—it may seem trivial, but in a high-stakes situation, protecting your space and your family's peace of mind is crucial.

Be Wary of Accountants with Referral Agreements

The world of accounting isn't always what it seems. Many accountants maintain referral agreements with IPs, receiving hefty fees to push clients into insolvency when better options may be available. I've seen it too many times: a well-meaning director trusts their accountant implicitly, only to be funnelled into a CVL by someone who stood to gain a nice payday. For a few thousand pounds, some accountants are willing to hand you off to the nearest IP, regardless of what's best for you or the business.

If your accountant suggests formal insolvency without exploring every other option, take it as a warning sign. An accountant should be a source of support, not a conduit to liquidation. Seek a second opinion if necessary, and be aware that not all advice is impartial—especially when a referral fee is involved. You deserve guidance from someone who prioritises your interests, not their own financial gain.

Remember, This Isn't the End

Directors facing a business downturn often feel like they've failed, like the walls are closing in, and there's no way out. But this is just one chapter, not the entire story. I've worked with directors who, after navigating a crisis, went on to build thriving businesses, learning from the struggles they faced the first time around. You took the risks, you built something, and that takes courage. Hold your head high and remember that this isn't the end—it's just a crossroads.

As much as they may try, don't let the system break your spirit. There's always another venture, another opportunity, and another day to get back in the ring. Keep moving forward, stay cautious, and protect yourself. And above all, avoid the insolvency trap that the industry is so eager to pull you into.

Thanks,

Patrick